The Ethical Protector

Essays on Police Ethics, Tactics and Techniques

Second Edition

By Jack E. Hoban and Bruce J. Gourlie

Edited by James V. Morganelli

The Ethical Protector

Essays on Police Ethics, Tactics and Techniques

RGI Media and Publications
Post Office Box 652
Spring Lake, NJ 07762
(732) 974-7582
www.rgi.co

Copyright © 2014, 2021
Jack E. Hoban and Bruce J. Gourlie

ISBN-10: 150081377X
ISBN-13: 978-1500813772

RGI Media and Publications is a division of Resolution Group International, LLC

On the cover: Sir Robert Peel statue by William Behnes; The Runaway photo (The Norman Rockwell Family Agency)

All rights reserved. No part of this book may be reproduced, distributed, or transmitted in any form or by any means, or stored in a database or retrieval system, without the prior written permission of the publisher. Special thanks to PoliceOne.com

Contents

Foreword		i
1.	An Ethics Model for LEOs	1
2.	The Ethical Protector	7
3.	Activating the Ethical Protector	10
4.	The Hunting Story	13
5.	Values, Morals and Ethics	21
6.	Are Ethics Tactical?	30
7.	Respectful Communication	37
8.	The Protector Discipline	53
9.	The Story of the Japanese Prisoner—Protecting Our Enemies	66
10.	Ethical Protector Leadership	71
11.	The Protector Mindset	76
12.	What's in a Name?	89
13.	"Seeing" the Tactical—and Moral—Space	93
14.	More Than the Sum of the Parts	99
15.	Philosophy Drives Actions	107
16.	Ethics Drive Tactics; Tactics Drive Technique	113

17.	Martial Skills	119
18.	Defensive Tactics Training	123
19.	Police "Militarization"	130
20.	Take a Break and Tell a Story	136
21.	The Warrior Creed	138
22.	A True Test of the Warrior Creed	144
23.	Presiliency: Combating PTSD and Moral Injury	150
24.	Training Camden: Creating an Ethical Protector Culture	165
Epilogue		178

Foreword

Some years ago, I traveled to the west coast for training at a weekend event led by Jack Hoban. You may know of Jack. If you do, consider yourself lucky. If this is the first you've heard of him, consider yourself lucky.

During one of the segments, I was called to the front and given the task of physically defending another person who was to be attacked. Now, I was a highly adept martial artist training since I was nine and even lived in Japan for several years studying with the very best teachers of my art. I was not concerned about getting physical with an attacker. The attacker should be concerned about being attacked by me.

A fellow stepped up and proceeded to attack my "protectee," at which point I interceded to use my 20-odd years of experience to handily dispatch him. I can remember feeling pretty satisfied as I loomed over the aggressor, now face down in the dust, and twisted him into an airtight submission. I probably wanted to impress Jack and anyone else watching. I remember that moment as well as I remember the next: Turning to my "protectee" to acknowledge his safety, I realized I couldn't find him! He'd been silently nabbed by an unknown second attacker—cue the laugh track and the fool. I could be thankful it had not been "real life."

Jack was the one who had (sneakily, I might add) arranged the abduction. He had nothing against me, he was simply taking advantage of the opportunity to teach a larger lesson. And I have never forgotten that lesson. It laid bare the one thing no professional ever wants to admit they possess—a weakness they weren't even aware they had. My ability to serve up martial skill when needed lacked the one thing truly necessary for right action: Clarity of what one *ought* to do. My job, my role, in that moment was not to attack the attacker. It was to defend the person I was supposed to safeguard. Protect his life. Be his protector.

With all my training and experience, one might think that I should have already known this; that it would be second nature, a given. It was not. And the truth is, it is not for many other professionals. In that crucial moment, I was convinced I was doing the right thing, but I was wrong. I was confused. I failed in my ethical duty.

After training and studying with Jack for some 15 years, working with him these past several, teaching conflict resolution to LEOs alongside the experts at Resolution Group International (including Bruce Gourlie), being inspired to achieve a master's degree in Ethics, and having now trained martial arts for more than 35 years, I cannot over-emphasize the value of philosophical clarity for the protector ethic. The best reason to study martial arts or defensive tactics inevitably brings us full circle to the originating purpose behind their ancient conception and ageless refinement: Protecting others. The clarity of this protector ethic is by far the most important lesson for the simple reason that it puts every other lesson in context. Protecting others is to protect oneself; protecting self and others is to *protect the value of life*.

It is no mistake that within the annals of martial history, the highest order of mastery has always been the ability to undo an enemy while sparing his or her life, if at all possible. And within the philosophic realm, the value of life is the absolute value that qualifies all other human values. What good are any of our relative values if they are twisted to violate the existence and dignity of even one human being?

The LEO "Ethical Protector" knows this. The protector ethic purges the confusion of moral ambiguity and offers an actionable ethic to reinvigorate ourselves, recalibrate our motivating purpose and challenge us to act in accordance with who we know we ought to be. Clarity of moral purpose leads to ethical action.

The authors' wisdom and talent to deliver these lessons is unsurpassed. Bruce Gourlie was an FBI Assistant Special Agent in Charge (ASAC), certified in firearms and Police instruction. He is a leadership instructor, a published author, a former US Army infantry officer and a long-time practitioner of martial arts. He now runs security at a large hospital in New Jersey.

Jack Hoban is president of Resolution Group International (RGI), a conflict resolution training company that works with military and law enforcement organizations. He served as a U.S. Marine Corps officer and is a Subject Matter Expert for the Marine Corps Martial Arts Program. Jack had the privilege of being mentored by Dr. Robert "Bob" Humphrey, a Natural Law sage, and Cold War conflict resolution expert, who first articulated the Dual Life Value Theory of human nature. Jack is also a long-time student of Japanese martial arts master Masaaki Hatsumi, and under Dr.

Hatsumi's tutelage, has become a true adept of the martial ways.

Mastering these two essential halves—philosophical clarity regarding our natural, life-protecting ethic, as well as the physicality required to protect it morally—places both Jack and Bruce in a particularly rare position and grants the rest of us an extraordinary opportunity to train and learn this clarity for ourselves.

The Ethical Warrior concept was developed and is practiced by the United States Marine Corps. It is transmitted to the Marines through the Marine Corps Martial Arts Program (MCMAP). The concept has been adapted for Law Enforcement and is referred to as the Ethical Protector concept.

But what exactly is a "warrior?" A warrior, as defined by the authors, is "a protector of self and others, all others, including the enemy if possible; killing only when necessary and justified to protect life."

THE ETHICAL PROTECTOR

There are those who think anyone who faces adversity of any kind is a warrior. The local football team in my area is called the Warriors, as is a professional basketball team in California. Are they really warriors? This from the Internet: "The Way of the 'Inner Warrior' is personal training for individuals who are willing and able to begin living a life dedicated to the evolution of their spirit." Huh? Clearly, there is plenty of confusion.

The easy answer is that a warrior is a person who fights in wars. The most famous definition of "war" is attributed to Prussian soldier and military theorist Carl Philipp Gottfried von Clausewitz (1780-1831): "War is the continuation of politics by other means." We don't know about you, but that definition is about a clear as mud to us. Here's one from Dictionary.com: "War is a conflict carried on by force of arms, as between nations or between parties within a nation..."

Look again at the definition above, especially the part, "between parties within a nation." That would seem to make LEOs eligible to be called warriors. Webster's defines warrior as, "a man experienced or engaged in warfare; a fighting man." LEOs may not be in a physical confrontation every day, but they are trained and prepared to fight. That would also seem to make LEOs warriors. They are definitely protectors. The good ones are Ethical Protectors.

This book is adapted from a series of articles written originally for LEOs on PoliceOne.com, but be assured, the lessons herein are timeless and immutable. They can, have, and will grant us clarity. Clarity for the protector in all of us.

– James V. Morganelli

1

An Ethics Model for LEOs

Law enforcement officers today face more stress and ethical challenges than ever. The training offered to meet these challenges often focuses on policies, procedures, and tactics. The ethical questions addressed in training are usually the legally enforceable ones, like conflict of interest, misuse of position, and accepting inappropriate gifts. Yet gaining the trust and cooperation of those we serve requires a more comprehensive view of ethics. The ability to deal efficiently and dispassionately with those we encounter, and to use force effectively and humanely when necessary, depends heavily on the law enforcement officer's personal ethics. A successful approach to ethical training robust enough to face this tough challenge was developed by the U.S. Marine Corps. Although the military mission of the Marines differs from that of local, state, or federal law enforcement, its ethical construct can offer very practical benefits for law enforcement and the communities they serve.

The harsh realities of the global war on terror forced the U.S. military to face their own unprecedented challenges. They were fighting a protracted war against an elusive enemy. The adversaries were enmeshed in a foreign civilian population who lived in fear of the terrorists but were also skeptical of U.S. involvement. This situation required an evolution in training. The Marines utilized the Marine Corps Martial Arts Program (MCMAP) to addresses some of the unique challenges of counterinsurgency. It based its approach on clarifying the concept of an "Ethical Warrior." The key idea: Marines who view themselves as Ethical Warriors, principled protectors of life, are better prepared to confront, survive, and live with the realities of modern combat. The Ethical Warrior, as defined by the Marines, is a "protector," who protects and defends their own life, the life of others, and all life, if possible.

This life protecting concept is universally consistent with law enforcement's obligation to "protect and serve." In addition to being consistent with a strategy to avoid unnecessary violence and killing, and to limit civilian casualties, a strong ethical foundation mitigates combat burnout. While more research needs to be done, indications are that MCMAP's combination of physical and moral-values training may decrease the severity of Post-Traumatic Stress Disorder (PTSD).

So, how do we apply the Marine Corps' Ethical Warrior approach to law enforcement? A law enforcement "Ethical Protector" views every life as a life to be valued, protected, and defended, regardless of race, nationality, economic, or legal status. When called upon to deal with someone engaging in criminal behavior, the Ethical Protector's first motivation is to protect all those he or she serves—the public—and that includes the criminal, if possible.

This vision may be particularly appropriate to community policing. The value of involving the community in police work has been well established. The success of this approach depends on creating effective relationships between the police and community organizations, and on developing a basic sense of trust and respect between officers and the public at large. One obstacle to developing trust is the tendency for the police and the community served to view each as the "other." Police in Salinas, California, recently started incorporating military counter-insurgency theory into their policing strategy as a way to win hearts and minds—all hearts and minds—including gang members. It is working.

Demonstrated respect for human equality is the key to bridging the divide between LEOs and the public. In addition, departmental morale grows when LEOs regain the noble feeling of being a protector.

The Ethical Protector

We must now address how the Ethical Warrior training can help officers gain:

1. Ethical clarity
2. Superior communication skills
3. Physical self-confidence

While functions like patrol, investigations, and responding to emergency calls take up most law enforcement time and resources, all law enforcement agencies offer training in defensive tactics. While not strictly characterized as martial arts, their physical elements could be integrated with values stories that demonstrate the Protector Ethic. Appropriate law enforcement stories could be identified that convey the lessons of valuing and protecting life. Uplifting and heroic stories resonate with most people and help inspire moral behavior.

Training sessions would not have to be long. But they would be scheduled regularly to sustain physical skill lessons. Most important, the stories could be woven into the actual training.

Imagine this: you are at roll call. After announcements, there is a short training exercise on un-holstering and re-holstering your weapon (or some other important physical skill). Then someone shares an inspiring story or anecdote about giving a helpful hand, or maybe even performing a life-saving action. Ten minutes – max. You're done and ready for work.

Law enforcement officers can reflect the best values of the societies they serve. A proper moral-physical training and sustainment regimen can activate a feeling of "nobility" in our officers, and perhaps, even help them avoid PTSD or burnout. The result will be more motivated officers, greater respect for the law enforcement profession and more effective policing for our communities.

2

The Ethical Protector

The desire to protect life is a natural human instinct. Almost everyone will fight to protect loved ones. Many people will even fight to protect a stranger—especially if there is no other choice. Law enforcement officers risk life and limb to protect their entire communities—their highest purpose is to protect others.

We believe Ethical Protectors protect *all* life, including the lives of criminals, whenever possible. If you ask LEOs why they signed up for the job, they might say, "...to put criminals in jail." But if one thinks about it, incarceration is a form of protection for the community. Although legal penalties may deter future criminal actions, the penal system can also serve the criminal by providing the opportunity for rehabilitation and redemption. Yet these functions are only part of the overriding goal to protect *all* of society.

Law enforcement officers make a conscious decision to dedicate their life to protecting others—all others, if possible—anywhere, anytime. This commitment deserves a title reserved for this noble tradition: Ethical Protector. Are other responders, such as paramedics, firefighters, emergency room doctors and nurses also protectors? Yes, and they are often heroes. But there is one important distinction: Although these others may risk their own lives to save others, they are not required to fight or even kill to protect life. The paradoxical-sounding statement, "protectors kill to protect life" differentiates the LEO from the other protector professionals who do not have the burden of application of force in their job description.

There is no more physically, mentally, or spiritually dangerous act a person can perform than a life-or-death struggle with another human being. Yet fighting for and possibly killing to protect life is a moral act. It is the noble duty and responsibility of the Ethical Protector.

3

Ethical Protector Development

The law enforcement profession requires devotion, sacrifice, and courage. LEOs in this noble field need a firm foundation of ethical principles worthy of those they protect. Ethics are rarely discussed in the context of leadership and even less well understood. But individual officers can pattern their behavior to become more ethical and also inspire more ethical leadership from above.

By the way, *all* police officers are leaders! The public looks to you to lead them safely out of a conflict situation.

We have devised a process to kickstart a broad understanding of the Ethical Protector concept:

The Ethical Protector

1. Calibrate your moral compass by clarifying and activating your own ethical understanding of human equality.

2. Develop an "Ethical Protector Self-Concept" by honestly applying an ethical foundation to all the personal and professional decisions within your power.

3. Develop a "Protector mindset" by training physically in defensive tactics and/or martial arts.

The first step in calibrating a compass is to locate a magnetic pole. The moral compass is no different. The moral compass reveals a standard by which all judgments, values, and actions can be assessed for their moral and ethical validity.

To this end, we must recognize one of the most important and unique phenomena of

MCMAP training: the recounting of stories with strong emotional impact that inspire moral behavior. Marines, and police officers, too, seem to respond best when these stories are "tied" to training. That is why we call our values stories "tie-ins." The realistic physical training and "tie-ins" work best in combination rather than separately—much better than a purely intellectual approach, such as a dry classroom lecture. The most unique and well-known tie-in is called "The Hunting Story." You will read it in the next chapter. It is a powerful way to recognize humanity's absolute value, the "Life Value," and its corollary, human equality.

4

The Hunting Story

The ancient Greeks said, "All actions derive from philosophy." The protector ethic is based upon a clear philosophy of values. The bedrock of that set of values is a single universal value. What is that value? Perhaps the best way to address the issue is to relate an experience of Robert L. Humphrey.

Humphrey was an Iwo Jima Marine rifle-platoon commander in World War II. He later went to work for the State Department during the Cold War. Humphrey's mission, during that delicate time, was to resolve a conflict between the U.S. and an allied country in Asia Minor. The future of a key U.S. installation in that country was in jeopardy due to unrest and rioting over our presence there. It seemed the local people, disillusioned with the character of the U.S. presence there, just wanted the Americans to go home.

Humphrey, trained as a lawyer and diplomat, began his task by surveying the opinions of both sides. Most Americans—including the ambassador—thought the locals merely wanted money from the U.S. government and would only truly be satisfied when all Americans paid up and left. In casual conversations with other Americans, Humphrey also learned many considered the local people to be, "stupid, dumb, dirty, dishonest, untrustworthy, disloyal, cowardly, lazy, unsanitary, immoral, cruel, crazy, and downright subhuman." No matter what he did, Humphrey couldn't stop the negative talk. Similar opinions of developing world people remain today. Some people have the same idea about folks in poor U.S. neighborhoods, for that matter.

A survey of the local population, however, yielded surprising and encouraging results. The issues the locals were voicing about the base were masking a different problem. Rather than wanting money or being unsupportive of the U.S.'s anti-Communist mission, the local people merely wanted to be treated with respect and dignity. Their perception was that the Americans did not view them as equal human beings.

Humphrey thought he had solved the problem. The Americans did not have to leave, or even give the locals more money. They only had to live up to the spirit of the U.S. Declaration of Independence and its notion that "all men are created equal." Humphrey was dismayed when his good news did not overcome the Americans' negative opinions. His colleagues could not see past the unfamiliar culture, customs and poverty which were a reality in that underdeveloped country. The diplomats were of no help. One said, "There's no such thing as human equality. Some people are tall, some people are short, obviously everybody is different." It seemed as if they either did not believe in human equality or didn't know what the term meant.

Humphrey was forced to ask himself what exactly "human equality" meant and how to teach Americans to respect all others as equal human beings. He searched high and low for an approach that worked. He finally found the answer in an unlikely place—the back of a truck in a poor rural village.

As a diversion from his job, Humphrey decided to go hunting for wild boar with some personnel from the American embassy. They took a truck from the motor pool and headed out to the boondocks, stopping at a village to hire some local men to beat the brush and act as guides. This village was extremely poor. The huts were made of mud and there was no electricity or running water. The streets were unpaved dirt and the whole village smelled awful. The men looked surly and wore dirty clothes. The women covered their faces, and the children had runny noses and were dressed in rags.

One American in the truck said, "This place stinks; these people live just like animals." Another said, "They just don't value life like we do." Finally, a young Air Force man said, "Yeah, they got nothin' to live for. They may as well be dead."

Then an old sergeant in the truck spoke up. He was a quiet man who never said much. In fact, except for his uniform, he reminded Humphrey of one of the tough men in the village. He looked at the young airman and said, "You think they got nothin' to live for, do you? Well, if you are so sure, why don't you just take my knife, jump down off the back of this truck, and try to kill one of them?"

Dead silence.

Humphrey was amazed. It was the first time anyone had said anything that had actually silenced the negative talk about the local people. The sergeant went on to say, "I don't know either why they value their lives so much. Maybe it's those snotty nosed kids, or the women in the pantaloons. But whatever it is, they care about their lives and the lives of their loved ones, same as we Americans do. And if we don't stop talking bad about them, they will kick us out of this country!"

Humphrey asked the old sergeant what we Americans could do to prove our belief in the peasants' equality. The sergeant answered, "You got to be brave enough to jump off the back of this truck, knee deep in the mud and sheep dung. You got to have the courage to walk through this village with a smile on your face. And when you see the smelliest, dirtiest *scariest* looking villager, you got to be able to look him in the face and let him know, just with your eyes, that you know he is a man who hurts like you do, and hopes like you do, and wants for his kids like we all do. That's the only way."

The Hunting Story has immediate and strong emotional impact. We sympathize with those poor villagers. Almost everyone has felt the pain and anger of disrespect. The people in that village weren't speaking out, but in their hearts each of them was saying, "Don't look down on me. You are my equal—my life and the lives of my loved ones are as important to me as yours are to you."

The Americans suddenly understood two things. First, no one would try to kill one of them because taking innocent human life is anathema to all moral people. Second, despite how worthless the villagers' life might appear, if attacked, any villager would have defended himself and his family with all his might. He cherished his life and the lives of his loved ones just as much as anyone else. At last, here was Humphrey's way to make the truth, "all men are created equal," truly self-evident.

Humphrey had great success relating this insight he called the "Life Value" to other military personnel at the U.S. base in formal presentations. However, he realized that he needed a way to sustain the feeling of human equality under the stress of danger and/or culture shock. Drawing on his own experience and relying on the nearly universal impulse for young servicemen to prove their courage and manhood, Humphrey offered free boxing lessons to anyone interested. He found that moral lessons were easier to teach when the students bonded through the combination of physical danger and fortitude necessary to excel at boxing.

It is vital to remember the exact words of the sergeant: "I don't know either why they value their lives so much. Maybe it's those snotty nosed kids, or the women in the pantaloons. But whatever it is, they care about their lives and the lives of their loved ones, same as we Americans do." Valuing one's own life is only half of the equation. The Life Value is a dual value—self and others. Ethical people have a good sense of how to keep that balance. There is no more important factor at any level of law enforcement than the duty to protect the community being served. A preeminent focus on this dual Life Value of self and others is an excellent moral basis upon which to build a sense of duty to "protect and serve" as a law enforcement officer.

5

Values, Morals and Ethics

Lifetimes have been devoted to the study of values, morals, and ethics. But for our purposes, we will confine ourselves to clarifying and activating those principles necessary to be an "Ethical Protector." We must understand how orienting to a moral magnetic north applies to our everyday conception of right versus wrong.

Gaining philosophical clarity—even for just the lexicon of the Ethical Protector—is a key step in activating a stronger, internal moral sense. That moral sense guides our actions under stress. *So, we must not skip this step!* We can also help people become ethical by encouraging them to act more consistently with their clarified moral values. That posits a question: "Why don't people act ethically in the first place?" Either consciously or subconsciously, people act based upon their core values. If we haven't clarified our personal philosophy—our core values—we may not know how to act ethically, particularly under stress. Philosophical confusion may even cause us to freeze at the most critical time.

Our emotions can also obscure our view of the Life Value as the one superseding and objective value. Fear, anger, shock, disgust, and grief, while natural and understandable reactions to immoral behavior, cannot be the only driver of our actions.

The Ethical Protector is a bit of a philosopher. He/she knows their values, combined with training, will almost certainly drive what they do on the street or on the battlefield.

Philosophical terms such as "values," "morals" and "ethics" are used rather imprecisely in our society. But it is especially important to understand the distinctions, particularly if you might be involved in violent or deadly situations.

To facilitate the development of the Ethical Protector concept while working with the U.S. Marine Corps and Law Enforcement, we created the following primer:

Values

According to Dictionary.com, values are, "things that have an intrinsic worth in usefulness or importance to the possessor," or "principles, standards, or qualities considered worthwhile or desirable." Values can be tangible (things) or intangible (beliefs, attitudes). Here is the critical point: although we tend to think of values as something good, virtually all values are "relative" — valuable to some, but not all. Almost all values are morally neutral until qualified by asking questions such as, "How is it good?" or "Good to whom?" The "good" can sometimes be just a matter of opinion or taste, or driven by culture, religion, habit, circumstance, or environment. Almost all values are relative values. The exception is the Dual Life Value of self and others identified in the Hunting Story in Chapter four.

The Life Value calibrates our moral compass. By applying the Life Value to relative values, we clarify the ethics of our actions. For example, courage is generally considered a great moral value. When a LEO rescues a passenger from a burning vehicle, he or she has performed a courageous act—risked his or her own life to save another's. But some people thought that flying planes loaded with passengers into buildings on September 11, 2001 also required "courage." However, only the first example is moral because it served to protect the Dual Life Value.

Morals

A relative value can become moral when it protects and respects the Life Value of self and others. The great moral values, such as truth, freedom, and charity, etc., have one thing in common: they are life-protecting or life-enhancing for all. But they are still relative. Our "moral" values must be constantly examined to make sure they are performing their life-respecting mission. In this context, even the Marine Corps core values of, "honor, courage, and commitment" require examination. "Courage" can wrongly be expressed as reckless martyrdom, "commitment" can sometimes become irrational fanaticism, and "honor" can be twisted into self-righteousness, conceit, and disrespect for others. Criminals believe in their own standard of "honor." We have all heard the saying "honor among thieves." They may face danger with "courage" and have "commitment" to their illegal ends. What then sets us apart? Respect for the lives of self and *all* others sets us apart.

Here is the basic principle: *a moral value, no matter how "great" cannot supersede the Life Value.* When it does, the trouble starts. Guaranteed.

Ethics

A person who knows the difference between right and wrong and prefers the right is *moral*. A person who *does* the right thing is ethical. *Ethics are moral values in action.* We strive to live morally because true ethics protect life and is respectful of others. It is a lifestyle that is consistent with humankind's universal values as articulated by the American Founding Fathers—human equality and the inalienable right to life. As Ethical Protectors it is our duty to be protectors and defenders of the Life Value and to perform the unique and difficult mission of protecting the lives of innocent people. This may extend to taking the lives of those acting immorally (acting counter to the Life Value) when necessary. To kill while protecting life is a hard thing, yet it is still moral. To kill because of religious, ethnic, or criminal values—all of which are relative—is unethical. It violates the Dual Life Value. Dedication to protecting the

Life Value of self and others—all others—makes the Ethical Protector different and moral.

Remember: ethics are moral values in action. A person who knows the difference between right and wrong and prefers the right is moral. A moral is a feeling or true sense of right and wrong. A person whose morality is reflected in a willingness to do the right thing, even if it is hard or dangerous, is ethical. An ethic is a correct, moral action.

It starts in the school yard. Most everybody knows the bully is wrong—that's morality. But only a few will speak up to protect the one getting bullied by calling for a teacher—that's ethics. Even fewer will step in physically to protect the child being bullied—that's the behavior of an Ethical Protector. Here is a story you can use to explain this point:

The Bully

You are a kid in the schoolyard.
You see a bully. He thinks he is the "top

dog." That is fine. That perception is his relative value.

But when his relative value supersedes the Life Value of another kid—when the bully picks on and/or physically hurts another kid—this is wrong and must be stopped. Here is the rule: *Relative values, no matter how "great," cannot supersede the Life Value*.

You see the bully picking on another kid. You feel in your gut that this is wrong. Congratulations, you are moral. By the way, most people are moral, they know the difference between right and wrong.

Now... you see the bully picking on another kid. You overcome the "freeze," the embarrassment, the reluctance to being called a snitch or tattletale, and you go tell a teacher. Congratulations! You are ethical. Ethics are moral values in action.

The Ethical Protector

Now... you see the bully picking on the other kid. You overcome the freeze, the fear, and you go to the aid of the kid being bullied. You put yourself at risk to protect another. Congratulations! You have the makings of an Ethical Protector.

And it sure does not end in the schoolyard. Almost all problems in our society are caused by bullies—those who would supersede the Life Value of others with their own relative values. We need Ethical Protectors to counter bullies. It is moral to understand it is wrong to attack an innocent person. But it is ethical to physically stop the attacker. LEOs conduct thousands of such ethical acts every day. These actions are often thought of as, "just doing my job," but are actually enormously powerful expressions of the Ethical Protector lifestyle.

6

Are Ethics Tactical?

"The Hunting Story" in Chapter Four tells how a simple soldier in the back of a truck activated a feeling of human equality between relatively well-off Americans and destitute villagers in a poor country with a few words and a challenge. When asked to articulate why all people feel their lives are equal, he said, "I don't know why they value their lives so much. Maybe it's those snotty-nosed kids or the women in the pantaloons. But whatever it is, they care about their lives and the lives of their loved ones, same as we do."

Human equality and the inalienable right to life underlie the Ethical Protector concept. All other values are relative, but the Life Value is absolute and universal. LEOs challenge criminal behavior—that's the job. We do not respect criminal values and behaviors. However, if we are true Ethical Protectors, we do respect the life of the criminal.

But that posits a few important questions: with so much emphasis on values, do we risk making LEOs "too ethical" to deal with immoral and dangerous criminals? Wouldn't it be better to only focus on protecting our own lives and the lives of the innocent? Don't we put ourselves at additional and unwarranted risk by trying to also protect the "bad guys?"

"Protecting criminals" is one of the most frequent concerns raised when applying the Ethical Protector concept to law enforcement. One critic wrote: "To start by believing that every bad guy deserves that level of respect just may be enough to slow down reactions at crucial times in 'kill or be killed' situations." This is an important issue. It could be a life-or-death issue. The last thing we want is to advocate a concept that will make LEOs less safe. In fact, if activating respect for the Life

Value of self and others—all others—could make protectors less safe, it in and of itself, would be immoral.

In the Marine Corps, we deal with this central question: Should Marines be trained as killers or protectors? Are "protectors" as prepared for the realities of war as "killers?" Will ethics training somehow make Marines "soft," and less capable of accomplishing the mission? When a Marine is in a fire fight with his sights on an insurgent who is shooting at him, will he suddenly freeze, say to himself, "that guy's life and the life of his loved ones are as important to him as mine are to me," and fail to pull the trigger? Even hesitate? We agonized over these points in MCMAP.

Law enforcement officers might very well ask themselves this same question. Many have conveyed to us that they have also considered this dilemma. Should police officers be trained primarily as "enforcers" or "protectors." Our Ethical Protector approach has even been called, "not aggressive enough." That was a first! With

Jack a Marine and Bruce a soldier, neither of us have ever been called not aggressive enough!

Finally, we arrived at the big question: Are ethics tactical? One of the definitions of the word "tactic" is: "A maneuver or plan of action designed as a way of gaining a desired end or advantage." What is the desired end if faced with taking a dangerous person into custody or ending a violent encounter? It is to accomplish the lawful action while protecting ourselves, innocent others, and the criminal, if possible. Of course, the desired end is not always possible. We may need to use appropriate force if the criminal poses an imminent threat. Force is not used just because we are following departmental rules and guidelines, but out of a genuine desire to protect life.

So, is being an Ethical Protector too soft or not? Anecdotally, we have heard both sides of the argument from sincere people who have, "been there." After a lot of thought, we still don't know the answer definitively, but imagine the following scenarios:

1. You are walking through a forest and you see a massive grizzly bear. Would you be afraid? Almost definitely so.

2. You are walking through a forest and see a grizzly bear with two cubs. Would you be less afraid or more? Most people would say, "more afraid." Why more afraid? Because even in nature, we know the protector is more dangerous than the killer.

The same seems to be the case in law enforcement. Obviously, good LEOs don't think of themselves as killers, but even if they only think of themselves as criminal-catchers, that perspective could very well lead to the self-image of "garbage man" collecting "human garbage." You may even think your approach needs to be just as ruthless as the criminal's, only "different." This, we believe, is a trap. Taking the "out thug the thug," approach can color our psyche in an extremely negative way. And it is not necessary. Protectors are more dangerous than thugs. We wholeheartedly believe this is due to their cause being purer and their actions being more committed.

But you must be good. Really good.

A *well-trained* Ethical Protector is not only more moral, but more psychologically and tactically powerful than a criminal. What could be more fierce than well-trained, ethical LE professionals engaged in the performance of their sworn duty to protect and defend the innocent people on their watch? We cannot think of anything. In fact, some of the earliest and most elite units in military history started as bodyguards to emperors and kings.

By the way, as you may have guessed, Marines don't hesitate to pull the trigger when it is necessary to protect their lives, the lives of their fellow Marines, and the lives of the innocent people in their area of operation. As an Ethical Protector, you will too.

7

Respectful Communication

Basic verbal de-escalation skills are being overlooked by too many police officers. Just look at the news. We see too many videos of fights we think would never have happened if the officers had been more skillful communicators.

One of the most important aspects in the development of the Ethical Protector concept largely came from the teachings of a great man who preached the concept of respectful communication.

Jack met George "Doc" Thompson, creator of the Verbal Judo Tactical Communication method, many years ago at an NYPD training. They became good friends. Doc Thompson was an accomplished scholar with a PhD, but he was also an experienced cop. His Verbal Judo techniques were developed and refined on the street. Doc passed away in 2011, but one of his right-hand men, Gary Klugiewicz, has polished and expanded upon many of the Verbal Judo principles through his company, Verbal Defense and Influence (VDI)[1]. Our organization, Resolution Group International (RGI), includes VDI training in all our Ethical Protector Certification Courses.

VDI has a lot to offer, and it is best to talk to Gary to learn more, but here are the four contact and de-escalation methodologies that we focus on at RGI that are based upon Doc's teachings:

1. **Universal Greeting.**
    1. Give an appropriate greeting.
    2. Introduce yourself.

---

[1] https://vistelar.com/in/training/

3. Give the reason for the contact.
4. Ask a relevant question.

You say, "Hi, good morning. My name is Officer Peterson from the Sea Lake Police Department. I noticed that your car is parked in a fire zone. Is there an emergency? Is everybody OK?"

If you are an experienced cop, you may start your contacts differently, but this is what we teach as a *basic*. This proven methodology has worked for decades. Do it this way, and your chances of having an easily manageable encounter drastically increase. Skip a step, and you open yourself up for a distracting and perhaps confrontational squabble. If you open with, "Is that your car?" and they reply, "Who wants to know?" "Why are you bothering me?" you could be on your way to a quarrelsome encounter. Try the Universal Greeting; it works.

Then, try...

2. Beyond Active Listening.
   1. Listen
   2. Empathize
   3. Ask to Clarify
   4. Paraphrase
   5. Summarize

He says, "No, officer, no emergency, I just want to run into the building to get something. I'll be right back." You listen, then say: "I understand, it's kind of a pain to park way over there in the parking lot. But there's no emergency, correct? That's good. So, you just wanted to run in and get something. Do I have that right?"

From there you could (Universal Greeting, continued):

- Ask for identification
- Ask for more information
- Make your decision
- Conduct an appropriate close

You say, "What's your name? Bill? OK, Bill, is there anything else I need to know? Because if that's the whole story, I am going to have to ask you to move your car and park in the lot before you go inside."

Bill: "OK, Officer, you're right, I was just in a hurry. I'll move it."

You: "Thanks, Bill, I appreciate it. Have a great day."

Do you really have to say all of that? We recommend you do, even if your script varies a little. At least make sure you cover all that ground. It may take a few seconds longer than what you usually say, but we know it works well. Unless, of course, they start to argue with you.

Then, try the...

3. Persuasion Sequence.
   1. Ask – Don't Tell
   2. Explain Why

3. Offer Options, Not Threats[2]
4. Give a Second Chance[3]
5. Take Appropriate Action

Instead of quickly complying, Bill says: "Hey, I'm only going to be here for a minute. There's no fire. I'll be out of here in no time."

You: "Right, Bill, I heard you. But I am asking you to move your car before you go in. Just in case."

Bill: "I could have been in and out by now."

You: "Bill, you seem like a reasonable guy. You wouldn't want to block the fire lane if you got held up inside for some reason and there was an emergency, would you? Your car would be blocking our emergency vehicles from getting in here. We need you to move it now."

---

[2] We offer three options: first a "good" one, then a "bad" one, then another "good" one.
[3] We typically say these *exact* words: *"Sir, is there anything I can say to get you to …? I would like to think so…"* They are time tested.

Bill: "Don't you have anything better to do? Stop harassing me."

You: "Look, I've asked you politely to move. I told you why. So now we have several options. Option one, you move your car—right over there to the parking lot—and then go about your business." Option two, I ticket your car and call a tow truck. That's the law and that's what I have to do if you won't help me out here. You don't want that, do you?" Doesn't it make more sense to just quickly move your car so we can both get on with what we need to do today?"

Bill: "Oh come on, give me a break, you're not going to tow me for this. I'll be right back."

You: "Unfortunately, if you walk away you will get a ticket and you will get towed, Bill, I've asked you, I've told you why, I gave you options: a couple of good ones, but also a bad one—for you. This is your last chance. Is there anything I can say to get you to work with me today and move that car? I'd like to think so...

Bill: "Oh, all right, I'll move it. *Harumph*."

Whew, that was a close one. But a little respectful and skillful persuasion has done the trick. And it works the vast majority of the time.

But, uh oh. Bill just turned around and is heading back.

"Forget it! Bite me, pig. I pay your salary!"

Whoa! OK, now what?

4. When Words Alone Fail.

Even the fantastic Persuasion Sequence doesn't work every time. People keep arguing anyway, or they may even physically attack you. It's time to stop talking when:

1. The Persuasion Sequence doesn't work or is inappropriate
2. You find your self engaged in excessive repetition or an argument
3. There is a personal safety issue
4. There is a threat to property

5. Something of a higher priority happens

It is now time to ACT!

It is important to know when words won't work, and it is time to do something. If talking isn't working—you are threatened, property will be damaged or there is an emergency that you must deal with—then you must act. In Bill's case, you will be giving him a ticket and calling a tow truck.

We think of skillful de-escalation language as a tactical assessment. If you are dealing with a suspect, and you get to step 3 or 4, what does that tell you? The research says that the vast majority of reasonable people will comply after step 1 or 2. Therefore, you know that you are dealing with an unreasonable, or maybe even dangerous, person. In other words, you have used the Persuasion Sequence to assess the tactical situation. At step 3 you are well-advised to get tactically prepared for a problem.

It seems simple, right? Well, not really. There is the protector mindset piece, as well. If tactical communication is used without sincere respect for the person you are dealing with (not respect for his attitude or behavior, but for his life as a human being), communication techniques are just techniques, not negotiating skill. Just reading the script above may come out forced or sarcastic or *dis*respectful. It is also not easy to talk this calmly and clearly under stress. Success comes from your presence, your tone, and your sincerity. It comes from *how* you say things as much as from the things you say.

In addition, having a set script in mind—even if it a script of your own—relieves you of the necessity to think about what you will say next in an escalating situation. You *know* what you will say next, and you can focus in on the tactical realities. Make *others* think about what they will say next, or think about how to answer *your* questions, rather than how they might get the jump on you.

OK, let's make things a little more serious with a scenario borrowed from our friends at VDI.

"The Distraught Gunmen"

I. The Scenario

A recently divorced man is driving through town with his 7-year-old daughter in the car when he sees his estranged wife travelling in her own car. He pulls alongside her and tries to get her to stop and speak with him. She refuses, speeds up and tries to drive away.

Infuriated, he follows her, eventually ramming her car into another car. He jumps out and fires three rounds from a pistol he is carrying into the side of the car.

You and your partner are called to the scene and see the distraught man standing outside the wife's car with his gun to his head. You are not entirely sure what is going on, but you (1) recognize the man, and (2) see the little girl in the other car.

What do you say to the man with the gun?

II. Utilizing the Persuasion Sequence

1. Ask – Don't Tell

"Sir, please put the gun down immediately and step away from it."

He refuses. [Note: Think about how your partner might reach the little girl in the car and move her to a place of safety]

2. Explain Reason Why

"Sir, I think I know you. Your name is Bill, right?"

"Bill, you know you are a danger right now, don't you? Let's make sure no one else gets hurt. There are innocent people all around this area. You wouldn't want to hurt anyone else, would you? I need you to put the gun down, now!"

He refuses.

3. Give Options (good/bad/good)

Bill, we have some options here. Option 1, which I think is the best one, is that you put the gun down immediately and we find out what is going on here, deal with it in the best way possible, so that no one else gets hurt.

Option two, is not so good. You have already fired that weapon and I cannot be sure that you will not fire it again. I can't let you do that. So, if you don't put the gun down, my partner and I have no choice but to shoot you. And we will.

Now we don't want to do that. Like I said, we don't want anyone else to be harmed. Certainly not innocent bystanders, and that could happen if you don't put your weapon down right now.

He again, refuses. It may launch into a diatribe, and what he says may or may not make sense. But the bottom-line is that he *must* put down the gun.

4. Second Chance:

"Bill, I have asked you to put that gun down so that we can talk this thing out. I've told you the options and I think we can agree that making sure everyone is safe makes the most sense. Please, I don't want to have to shoot you. Is there anything I can say to get you to put the gun down right now? *I would like to think so..."*

Again, he refuses.

5. Act!

If you sense that you are making no progress with Bill, you must act at this time. Depending on the distance, your skills and confidence, etc., you must move to eliminate the threat by taking down the gunman, Bill. Act decisively and as safely as possible under the unique situation.

As I am sure you realize, it may be a bit unrealistic to think that an actual scenario like this would be resolved as quickly as we have written it here. And we certainly hope that Bill does eventually put the gun down so no one gets hurt. Our purpose is merely to re-iterate the VDI script with some additional context. It may also suggest some options—and a tactical de-escalation script—to have in your mind should you find yourself in a similar situation.

Could the Persuasion Sequence be a tool to help you organize your approach to this kind of scenario? Your call. But whatever you say in a conflict situation is best said with a protector self-concept in mind. Your tone and ability to project empathy is important, too.

One of our RGI associates, James Shanahan, was a veteran NYPD trainer and hostage negotiator. He describes the two extremes of how two kinds of cops handle a "situation:"

1. One cop can talk a foaming-at-the-mouth rabid dog off a meat truck.
2. Another cop could show up at the scene of the blessed nativity and end up splitting somebody's head open.

Where do you fall along the continuum between cop #1 and cop #2? Again, respectful communication tactics may seem like a lot of trouble to go through just to get someone to move their car. But they will make your day easier and may keep your agency from getting complaints. They might even keep a real bad guy from having an excuse to fight you.

In any case, the VDI respectful communication tactics are great for new folks on the force who are not used to thinking on their feet—but, also worth a review by the veterans. By the way, the Persuasion Sequence also works great on teenagers. Option 2? Take away their phone. They hate that.

Please consider these VDI-RGI respectful communication ideas. Could you work with us on that? We'd like to think so!

8

The Protector Discipline

The Ethical Protector law enforcement officer protects lives. That includes, of course, the lives of the citizens they serve, but also the lives of criminals, whenever possible. This is doing more than what is legally required when protecting those under arrest or serving a sentence. It is an ability and commitment to look past people's behavior—legal or illegal—and see the intrinsic Life Value behind that behavior and respect it. This is important for two reasons:

1. It is logical.
2. It is psychologically healthy for you.

The Life Value is a universal and absolute value—we all value it, or we would not be alive.

It defines our human equality. Therefore, it is logical to treat everyone as an equal based on their Life Value, even if their behavior does not meet acceptable standards. In fact, the ability to separate the absolute value of life from the relative value of behavior—respecting the former while appropriately addressing the latter—is critical in resolving conflict. We call it The Protector Discipline.

Regarding our contention that everyone's life deserves to be valued, a reader commented, "One of the problems that we have in our society is that we respect those who are not deserving of respect." We could not agree more! But with some clarifications. We reject the moral relativism so prevalent in our generation's "thinkers." The assertion that all relative values are equal, simply different, and that we must give unconditional respect to values which are morally objectionable, is philosophically invalid. We think it is appropriate to apply judgments like "moral," "immoral," "right" and "wrong" to human behavior. But what is the logical and objective reference point from which to make that judgment?

Some behaviors are easy to judge. Acts clearly based on greed, cruelty, and cowardice are simple to condemn. However, it is more difficult to judge acts based on the misfiring of seemingly positive values. For example, most of us would agree that "honor" is a positive value. But consider the following: What if a teenage girl in a traditional society is killed by her own family for kissing a boy in public? They would call it an, "honor killing." We call it murder. Which is it?

As we discussed earlier, a value like honor is a relative value, morally neutral and understood in different ways by different people. It can inspire moral or immoral behavior. The key is to use the Life Value as the reference point for judging whether any relative value—even a great value like honor—is moral. The Life Value is the one value that cannot be trumped by any other relative value. In a nutshell, we must treat the Life Value as an objective, qualifying value which is always respected.

How do we know when a value is moral? The answer is simple in theory if not in practice: Values and the behaviors they inspire are moral when they promote the respect and protection of life and immoral when they do not. We could easily agree the relative values of criminals may be thoroughly immoral, but we would still protect their lives, if possible. After all, which is the worse crime:

- Stealing a car?
- Selling dope?
- Robbing a bank?
- Treating someone like a subhuman?

If we treated life as just another relative value or behavior, there would be no philosophical difference between the good guys and the bad guys.

If you think about it, there is an entire segment of our society whose behavior is so objectionable that it is sometimes hard to view these people as humans. They can be dirty, smelly, sloppy, lazy, argumentative, and disrespectful. They often lie and complain. Their behavior is sometimes immoral and even illegal. Yet, we love them unconditionally. Yes, I am talking about teenagers.

The reason we can abhor some teenage words and actions, yet still love them, flows from our ability to separate in our minds the relative value of their behaviors, which can be good, bad or indifferent (depending, sometimes, on the moment!), and the absolute value of their lives and our love for them, which is not relative. When my teenager acts objectionably or even criminally, I need not respect his behavior; but I still love him and respect his life.

As a protector professional "all" we have to do is extend that same disciple to others, all others. Respecting their lives while dealing professionally with their sometimes unlawful behaviors.

Dealing with criminals is obviously not the same as dealing with teenagers, although sometimes we are dealing with the same thing. It may seem ridiculous to say that we "love" a criminal but detest his behavior. Yet loving one's enemy is exactly what many religions advocate.

This little piece of philosophical clarification might be just what we need to act ethically and professionally under stress. We deal with the behavior, but we don't dehumanize the person. It can be exceedingly difficult to witness the illegal and immoral actions of a criminal and still separate the relative value of their behavior from the absolute value of their life. But it is the right thing to do. And it's a discipline – the Protector Discipline. It also may be one of the keys to avoiding stress, burn-out, and PTSD. For when we denigrate the value of one life, we denigrate the value of all life—including our own.

Perhaps this idea of respecting the value of life vs. the value of behavior can be brought home by asking yourself these questions:

Are there richer people in the world? Smarter? Better looking? More highly educated? Nicer? Done more good works than you have? Perhaps. But does that make their life worth more than your life? Certainly not to you! Life is an absolute value; all of the others are relative.

Respecting people as human beings – even if you don't respect their behavior – is also the key to de-escalating conflict. And safer, more tactical. Would you like to greatly increase the chance that a suspect resists arrest and fights you? Easy. Treat him or her disrespectfully.

Respect for human equality is also psychologically safer for the protector professional. Constant exposure to illegal and immoral behavior tempts us to dehumanize anyone not perceived to be in our "in-group." This "us versus them" mentality often exists, not only between LEOs and criminals, but between LEOs and citizens. It is now well established that dehumanizing "outsiders" is a major cause of Post-Traumatic Stress Disorder (PTSD) and cross-cultural conflict.

We are talking about our long-term psychological and spiritual health here, not only the immediate condition of life and limb after a confrontation. We all have friends who escaped conflicts without physical scars but could not escape the non-physical ones. This phenomenon has been noted in the military for many years and is now referred to as Post-Traumatic Stress Disorder.

Many of our veterans returning from Iraq and Afghanistan exhibit these symptoms. A study of Vietnam War veterans for more than 40 years yielded the observation that PTSD is an unfortunate, maybe inescapable, consequence of war—not a character flaw. Yet, in his book, "Achilles in Vietnam," clinical psychiatrist Jonathan Shay discusses dehumanization and disrespect for the enemy as a prime cause of PTSD.

The lesson for LEOs is obvious. Officers, too, are vulnerable to PTSD from one or more intense life-threatening engagements, as well as the chronic stress that comes from daily exposure to troubled people, helpless victims, and a constant undercurrent of conflict and danger. Not to mention community and departmental politics! But there are things we can do to make ourselves more resistant to the inevitable stress of conflict. We suggest that respect for the enemy (or criminal) as an equal human being—even though his or her behavioral values may be immoral—is essential in mediating PTSD.

It is important that we never lose sight of the fundamental value of every human life, especially the life of those whom we protect and even those who seek to harm us. We believe that dehumanizing our adversaries, as individuals or groups, is corrosive to our own respect for the Life Value. In other words, just as the literature suggests, dehumanizing others is dangerous to our own physical, mental, and spiritual health.

It may be helpful to explore why it is so tempting and seemingly natural to dehumanize our adversaries. For millions of years, human beings lived in small bands. Imagine a tribe — we'll call them Tribe A of Valley A — settled in a defensible geographic location with just enough food, water, and shelter to support their fairly small group. Tribe A is not particularly warlike, but they fiercely guard their limited resources.

Over in Valley B, Tribe B has a problem. They no longer have enough food in their territory, perhaps due to population growth, fires, droughts, or floods. Tribe B starts to roam and eventually they begin to encroach on Tribe A's territory. This is a serious life and death conflict. Tribe A must stop the "invasion" to protect the resources needed by its "in-group." Tribe A fights and kills to protect the resources that support their lives.

Yet, the people in Tribe A are not natural born killers of humans, just as we are not today. Think about it. Even in police work, how many natural born killers do we encounter compared to the rest of us non-killers? In fact, for virtually all of us, protecting life is our primary and universal value. So, what do the people in Tribe A do? How do they deal with the problem? They create an artifice: They allow themselves to *believe* that those "others" from the encroaching tribe are not human. They dehumanize them.

Now it becomes slightly easier to attack, and if necessary, kill them. It is an imperfect trick, but it works in the short term, when emotions like fear, anger, and disgust overwhelm reason. The artifice does not always work completely. People often feel guilty or depressed after they dehumanize others, especially if it results in violence and killing. But the sad truth is that we have been doing it for thousands of years. And we are still doing it.

People don't have to be of a distinctly different tribe to have conflict. Almost any real or imagined cultural or behavioral value deemed objectionable by one group can lead them to rationalize acts that violate the Life

Value of "others." People do it over such arbitrary differences as a favorite sports team. San Francisco Giants fan Bryan Stow was nearly beaten to death in the parking lot of Dodger Stadium reportedly for wearing a Giants jersey. The attackers didn't appear to care that they might kill Stow—a paramedic—they only saw an enemy from another "tribe."

We see how easy it is to dehumanize people just because they are not from our "in-group." It is even easier to dehumanize them when the culture or behavior of that other group is threatening, immoral or illegal—such as that of a criminal "tribe" or gang. It is easy to succumb to the seductive mistake of using relative values (behavior) rather than the Life Value (an absolute, universal value) as criteria for judging the worth of their life. When a person's behavior is not "equal," or does not conform to what is considered "good," then it is as if the person himself is not equal or worthy. When people of one relative value system (behavior, culture, religion, etc.) see people of another relative value system as "unequal" or sub-human, the trouble begins; and it could be big trouble.

LEOs are often susceptible to losing sight of everyone's Life Value. They deal repeatedly with difficult and dangerous people from identifiable ethnic, socio-economic, and neighborhood groups. It is all too easy to see these people as group members first, and human beings second. Even more because that is how they often see themselves.

To "inoculate" us to the dangers of dehumanization and PTSD, Ethical Protectors resist the "tribal artifice" in order to stay mentally and spiritually healthy. Ignoring the value of an adversary's life can be seductively easy, helping us to cope day-to-day in the short run. But in the long run, we can survive the most difficult situations with mind, body, and spirit intact by maintaining the Protector Discipline, and respecting all life, and dealing with immoral or illegal behavior as a separate and manageable part of the job.

9

The Story of the Japanese Prisoner: Protecting Our Enemies

Most of us know well of the World War II battle on the island of Iwo Jima—perhaps because of the famous flag-raising photo. But one of the dirty little secrets of that battle was that no one took prisoners. The Japanese did not believe in taking prisoners—surrendering, even when wounded, was wrongly considered a violation of the warrior code of *Bushido*. Unfortunately, some of our Marines began to follow suit with the killing of wounded, captured, or even surrendering Japanese soldiers.

One day on patrol, Dr. Robert Humphrey, years before he would be changed by the events in the "The Hunting Story," was a Marine rifle platoon lieutenant on Iwo Jima. On this day, he and his men came upon a young, emaciated Japanese soldier in a torn, filthy uniform emerging from a cave waving a white flag. This, in and of itself, was unusual as Japanese soldiers rarely surrendered. One of the Marines on the patrol, convinced that this was some kind of trick, raised his rifle to kill the boy.

But Humphrey found himself ordering the Marine to put down his weapon. A short, intense confrontation occurred between him and the Marine. The Marine was going to shoot that boy dead, Humphrey's order be damned. But discipline prevailed and the Marine lowered his weapon. As it happened, the Japanese soldier's surrender was genuine, and he was taken safely to the rear. The prisoner even turned out to be of some intelligence value.

Humphrey thought little of the incident at the time, there was so much killing before it and so much afterward. Yet nearly fifty years later, when asked to share his proudest achievement, it was that moment he cited:

On Iwo Jima, it was life or death every minute of every day. There was unavoidable killing every day. When I saw that Japanese boy trying to surrender and understood that this was perhaps the only time that I didn't have to kill, I took the opportunity. I believe that action saved my humanity.

Like most Iwo Jima veterans, who survived, I was deeply affected by the experience. Yet I never suffered the profound depression and shell-shock (PTSD) that some of the others did. I attribute it to saving that boy's life. Protecting my enemy, if you will.

There is a saying, "detest the crime, but respect the criminal." This perspective is not only for the benefit of the criminal, but also for us. There are negative consequences when we judge the value of people's lives solely by their relative cultural, behavioral, or even criminal values.

Is all life worth respecting? Yes. Life is an absolute and equal value. Behaviors are not necessarily to be respected; they are relative and need not be honored if they are disrespectful of the lives of others.

Will respecting the value of an opponent's life lead to confusion and delay in a violent confrontation? We don't think so, for two reasons. First, the Life Value is a dual value: Self and others. Protecting your own life is equally important. The value of the aggressor's life does not negate or decrease the value of your life. There is no reason to hesitate if you reasonably believe your life is in danger. Second, activating and clarifying the Life Value in advance will give you the confidence to act decisively, secure in the knowledge that you are acting as an Ethical Protector.

We can enhance our own effectiveness (and our lives) by showing a consistent and sincere respect for everyone we encounter—citizens and suspects—and having the guts to be friendly and nice to every person we meet. This means getting out of our vehicles and taking off our sunglasses (as Marines have been directed to do in their counterinsurgency efforts in Iraq and Afghanistan) and connect with your community. It is a little harder, maybe even a little more dangerous at times, but it makes for a better life. Everywhere you go, people will feel safer because of your presence. Being a true Ethical Protector brings serenity, nobility, and satisfaction—it's a better life.

LEOs serve daily in a jungle full of "experts" in criminal behavior and moral gray areas. But the Life Value is the "true north" of the moral compass that can keep officers on track. When we possess a calibrated compass, we can more reliably navigate that jungle. Without trying to gloss over the very real fact that Ethical Protectors may need to use force, we can articulate clearly that force is only to be used to protect life.

10

Ethical Protector Leadership

The law enforcement profession requires devotion, sacrifice, and courage. LEOs and those chosen to supervise others in this noble field need a firm foundation of ethical leadership worthy of those they lead. Yet, lack of effective leadership is a common problem across the law enforcement spectrum.

We have devised a process to kick start development of Ethical Protector leadership:

1. Calibrate your own moral compass by clarifying and activating your own ethical understanding.

2. Demonstrate the behaviors of an "Ethical Protector" by honestly applying an ethical foundation to all the professional decisions within your power.

3. Develop a "Protector mindset" by training physically in defensive tactics and/or martial arts.

4. Act as if your boss is already committed to steps one and two.

You can take the first three steps yourself. The critical fourth step is a way you can influence your boss to lead from a more ethical perspective.

Most law enforcement professionals have an initial positive reaction to the Ethical Protector message. However, the compliments are often followed by, "I have to function in the real world. My bosses only care about their career, covering their rear-ends, and looking good for their bosses. I try to do the right thing, but what can I do if my ethics conflict with their priorities?" A good question, but not one confined just to the front-line officer. Managers at all levels—and in all professions, for that matter—express similar frustration about their bosses. Is there a way to break through this seemingly universal obstacle?

One potentially powerful technique is to act as if the boss is an Ethical Protector already. This is the fourth step set forth above. The idea of "act as if" is a staple of the self-help vocabulary. Act as if you are confident, rich, or attractive and people will start treating you like the person you want to be. Once people perceive you differently, you might start to acquire the traits you most desire. This is an interesting theory, but what if we apply the same technique to others instead of ourselves? What if we apply this technique to inspire ethical leadership? Could we act as if our boss is operating from the same Ethical Protector perspective and frame our conversations along those lines when confronted with potential conflict?

For example, we may anticipate that our boss expects us to exaggerate certain statistical accomplishments to exceed organizational goals. Honesty in law enforcement reporting is a moral value because it contributes to an accurate assessment that facilitates effective policing and protects lives. Rather than ignoring the problem, or just complaining to our peers, we could have a conversation with our boss that assumes a common ethical understanding. One approach would be, "I know you want these statistics reported honestly and that our integrity matters more than any single report, so I'll be reporting numbers a little lower than you expected."

You may have a boss who will tell you they do not care about honesty or integrity, but one hopes that would be a very rare occurrence in law enforcement. It is more likely that framing the conversation in ethical terms will help clarify and activate the moral inclinations of your boss.

You may be hesitant to try the bottom-up "act as if" technique, so start small. Identify lesser issues that you can use to form the basis of your reputation as an Ethical Protector. These timeless values have a power of their own that can be a highly effective ally. You will likely find that your boss is trying hard to be ethical within the context of the unique pressures of his or her own position. Your spoken confidence that they will make the ethical choice may be just what they need to reinforce their resolve. Of course, you will only be able to pull this off if you are genuinely committed to being an Ethical Protector yourself.

11

The Protector Mindset

A protector mindset—the ability to act effectively and ethically under adversity—is key to being an Ethical Protector. Being effective under stress requires the ability to overcome emotional and autonomic impulses that might keep us from performing well in combat, or even get us killed. Our perspective is that clarified ethics makes you more effective and safer in a combat situation. After all, what are ethics, but moral (life-protecting) values in action?

One popular phrase says: "Be polite and professional, but have a plan to kill everyone you meet." It may sound sensible to some and cool to others, but both perspectives may fail to examine what that really means. What is the mindset of the person who adopts this philosophy? Is it that of a protector or that of a killer? Let's consider rewriting this popular phrase as: "Be polite, be professional, but have a plan to protect myself and all others I meet, if possible."

One of our challenges when we are called upon to train Marines for combat and police officers for service in some of the most dangerous cities in America is may we have a very short amount of time to give these warriors and protectors a sense of things it took us literally years to figure out. We try to create mental metaphors and easy physical drills that might give them a shortcut to grasping a sense of important concepts we have spent a lifetime learning. We'd try anything if it might make them personally safer and better protectors of others.

Maybe, we are a little successful. Sometimes. In truth, although the feedback we get is good, we can never be sure.

One of the things we talk about is how to train one's mind for dangerous situations, in other words, develop a Protector Mindset. We aren't talking about learning new information, but how to actually make the brain more efficient and resilient under stress. We've run our theories by some people who are experts in the science of the mind, including brain specialists, and we believe our theories are worth consideration and additional research.

Let's start off with the familiar theory of the "human trinity." It is said that we are made up of three parts: mind, body spirit. The spirit part consists, we think, of all the things that make us alive, or in the case of warriors and protectors, keeps ourselves and others alive. It is the will to live, as well as the calling to know ourselves as the protector of others. It is the fighting spirit and the will to survive. All of these things and many others that are hard to articulate but are felt.

The physical is easier to put into words. It's our bodies and what we do with them, also our environment. For warriors and protectors, it is our training and, ultimately, our actions.

But the mental... You can say it pertains to what goes on in our brain, what we think, or what we study and learn. But our research indicates it may be way more than that. Especially, as it pertains to our protector calling, and dealing with stress, uncertainty, and violence.

We think it goes without saying that we now know more about the functioning of the human brain, particularly under stress, than our warrior forefathers did. Consider the following illustration.

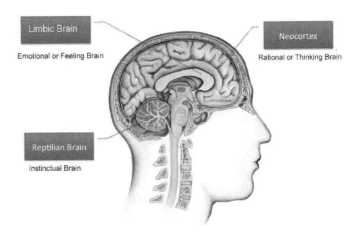

The brain is certainly much more complicated than this, but for our purpose of trying to understand the "mind" piece of the human trinity, we see that the brain is made up of three basic parts or functions. We have the stem or "reptilian" part of the brain. It is the "oldest" part of the brain and it controls our autonomic functions (breathing, heartbeat, etc.), as well as our "instinct-like" behaviors—fight or flight, for example. It can be very important for our survival but can't always be relied on to make optimal choices under confusing conditions.

Then we have the limbic part of our brain. It's where our feelings and emotions come from. It is a very important part, obviously, but it is not always rational.

Last, we have the neocortex, or as the name suggests, the "newest" part of the brain. This is where we can solve complex problems and make rational decisions. Its power is what separates us from the reptiles and even the other bigger-brained mammals.

So, which one serves us best as protectors in stressful and/or dangerous situations? Well, we need all three parts, certainly. We need the autonomic and survival skills of the brain stem. We need the feelings and emotions of the limbic brain, as they may be our connection to the "spirit" part of the mind-body-spirit trinity.

But it is the neocortex, and the ability to access it under stress, that is ultimately the most vital functioning area of the brain for warriors.

We'll use an example. Getting caught in an ambush. Tactically and (this is important) counter-intuitively, when ambushed you must attack toward and through the ambusher, collapsing the tactical space. What does your reptilian brain want to do? That's right, it wants to flee: you are being attacked, run! How about the limbic brain? It's not helping, its screaming, "we're all gonna die!"

And if you listen to either of those brains, the limbic is right. You're gonna die. So, you need to somehow override them. I call it toggling. You need to toggle "forward" to your neocortex, because the secret to your survival in this deadly situation is to do the counter-intuitive thing. You must press forward. Not run. Nor freeze and go all emotional. Attack! And the warrior or protector, when he or she has trained properly, has this ability to toggle into the cool, detached, problem-solving part of the brain. And for the vast majority of us, it isn't even a little bit easy. Not under stress. It takes practice, practice, practice. Mind-numbing repetition. But even that is just a metaphor, because only two-thirds of the brain goes numb. The other third, the neocortex, sharpens. Things slow down, things become clearer. That is the combat mindset. The protector mindset. If you are not aware of this process, if you don't, then, practice consistently and repetitively, you cannot expect to be able to toggle swiftly and effectively (and survive) in the event of a violent attack.

In the Marines (and maybe in your police academy) we did the most simple things over and over: draw, aim and dry fire weapons, change magazines, experience hardship, adversity and loud noises. Over and over and over. That's why most Marines and many officers, when the real thing happens, can toggle into that place in the brain where their training is stored. And act!

OK, what if you have never had Marine training or something similar? Let's talk about just your average everyday training. Here's maybe a more accessible example. Leverage. You are doing an arm bar. It's not working. You panic. Maybe you wish you could just disappear (brain stem), or get frustrated, angry and/or embarrassed (limbic). You freeze your feet and try to muscle it until it works. But it doesn't. Your partner is too big or too strong (or a jerk). Fail.

Why? Because your brain stem and limbic brain don't do levers. Levers are counter-intuitive. Push down to lift something up. Pull up to force something down. Left is right. Right is left. A powerful, powerful tool. Levers are something only a human being, with a neocortex, can imagine, much less use.

"Give me a place to stand, and a lever long enough, and I will move the world." Archimedes of Syracuse said that. He was a Greek mathematician, physicist, engineer, inventor, and astronomer.

We can't say that this is the most scientific explanation of how the mind works under stress and why slow, repetitive, accurate practice is vitally important for the warrior and protector. But We believe this idea to be fundamentally sound, and it is important to grasping what is meant by "mind," in the "mind-body-spirit" trinity.

This ability to toggle, we also believe, may be a key to understanding—and moderating—the tendency to de-humanize others who are not of our "tribe," like criminals.

We seem to be inordinately protective of our feelings and relative values, often irrationally fearing or detesting people who are different from us. We see this phenomenon between people of different colors, races, religions, political views, etc. We sometimes see great hate and even violence between followers of different sports teams. It's not new, but why is this?

It's because when we see people who are "not of our tribe," we have hundreds of thousands of years of experiences embedded in our DNA, brain stem and limbic brain that whisper to us: "Danger, danger. Must fear, hate, despise, de-humanize. It's the only safe way." And for thousands of years that may have been true. But not necessarily so. And we can now figure out if this "other" person is really a danger or not—if we choose. But not without our neocortex. It requires a counter-intuitive "toggle." "Wait, I see that he is another color, or speaks differently, or prays differently, or is wearing the jersey of my team's archrival, or is acting in a way I feel is immoral or I know is illegal." But think. Use that neo-cortex. Analyze the tactical situation. Observe their behavior.

Are they really a danger? Must I disrespect, demonize or dehumanize him?"

Maybe not. But it takes practice. Here's some homework. The next time you see a person that is obviously "not of your tribe," and who you ordinarily (admit it!) might instinctively dislike or distrust, see if you can take a second and toggle to that problem-solving part of your brain and re-evaluate. Stay and aware and tactical, but see how long it takes you to toggle. You may be able to see that person in a different way. Of course, they could possibly be dangerous, but maybe not. Let your neocortex decide. Now practice.

And check this out! Guess which part of the brain is most effected by stress? The limbic part. When you experience a disturbing event, a signal is sent that causes a fear response in the limbic brain, especially. People with PTSD tend to have an overactive response to stressful events. When the limbic brain is overactive, it's hard to think rationally. It is your neocortex that helps regulate emotional responses triggered by the limbic brain. An unregulated limbic brain combined with an underactive prefrontal cortex creates a perfect storm for PTSD. Without the ability to toggle out of the limbic brain into the neocortex, you not only set yourself up for tactical failure, but you also risk post-traumatic stress!

Can we further develop our Protector Mindset through toggling? Try it. We think it is a recipe for a safer and less stressful career and life.

12

What's In a Name?

Many readers agree that terms like "Ethical Warrior" and "Ethical Protector" do indeed apply to law enforcement officers, although some have commented that they didn't care what they were called, they just wanted to do the job well. Fair enough.

As we are talking about names, let us think about the term "law enforcement officer."

Do you like it? Do you think it is an appropriate and accurate description of what we do? You might ask, "Who cares?" But as amateur warrior philosophers, we know that words mean something.

So, what does the term "law enforcement officer" denote? It denotes a person who enforces laws, right? Sure, we do that, but is that who we are?

When you were a youngster and someone asked you what you wanted to do when you grew up, did you answer, "I want to enforce laws?" When you graduated from the academy and first put on that badge and gun, did you say to yourself, "OK, now let me get out there and enforce some laws!"?

We suspect that, even if you did not have the words for it, you envisioned yourself as a protector of people not just an enforcer of laws. You would be the "good guy," the community's "knight in shining armor." Sure, it sounds a little silly and naïve after many years on the job. But, admit it, many of us started off with that romantic view of life in the military or as police officer.

So, is "law enforcement" really the best way to describe our work?

The term law enforcement encompasses two major concepts: law and force. It bears repeating that the use of force—even lawful force—can have profound psychological consequences for the officer.

One of the temptations is to start viewing everyone as a potential aggressor. This may seem like a prudent and tactically sound approach. If we assess everyone's potential danger to us, we will be ready for any confrontation. The innocent people will never know the difference, and nobody gets hurt.

What is wrong with that?

The problem is that treating everyone as a potential threat is not what we signed up to do. The classic police motto is, "to protect and serve."

It is difficult to view everyone as a potential aggressor and still convey a genuine sense of concern to the people we are sworn to protect and serve. The officer can eventually begin to feel isolated and disconnected from the community. It's easy to imagine this becoming a self-reinforcing negative cycle. The result is a community who doesn't trust us—and a miserable, "burnt out" existence for us.

We are not suggesting law enforcement is a negative term. We are suggesting that officers should continually take the time to examine their attitude toward the work and compare it to their original motivation and to the broader concept of an Ethical Protector.

How about you? What is your deep down, fundamental self-concept? Enforcer? Or protector who is sometimes called upon to enforce? We think clarifying our own self concept is important for knowing what we will do under stress. It also makes us more resilient to that stress.

If we see ourselves as protectors—or even as Ethical Warriors—we can start referring to ourselves as such and maintain the motivation we entered this profession with.

Our old friend, the late George Thompson, liked to use the term "Peace Officer."

What do you think?

13

"Seeing" the Tactical—and Moral—Space

The Protector Mindset is the combination of physical training, mental toughness, and tactical awareness clarified by ethical life-protecting values. How is mental toughness measured? We can easily think of objective standards for physical fitness, tactical skill, and ethical knowledge. We generally think of "mentally tough" people as those able to endure difficult situations calmly and effectively without suffering serious psychological damage. It seems reasonable to view a combination of increasingly challenging training and practical experiences to be the route to toughness. But what does it mean to be tough? How do you know you will be tough enough when the critical incident happens?

Human beings are emotional. While most professionals keep their emotions under control during routine events, the prospect of physical conflict can quickly upset one's composure. Excitement, anger, and fear are all natural, but potentially unhelpful reactions to physical danger. Is toughness the ability to rid oneself of these emotions? Is a protector mindset an emotional blank slate? We think not. Rather, we believe the answer lies in the concept of "seeing the space."

The best way to understand this concept is to begin in the tactical realm. In any physical encounter there is a safest place to be. There may not be a completely safe place, but there are safer places than others in any given situation. We define "safest" as the physical and mental place where you are simultaneously the most tactically effective and in the least danger from your opponent. Interestingly, this spot is usually safer for the opponent too, inviting them to surrender peacefully. Because conflicts are dynamic, the safest place changes moment by moment as the details of the struggle unfold. "Seeing the space" means identifying where the safest spot is (the space where you gain the tactical advantage) and maneuvering along a safe path to that spot.

This principle holds true in any encounter, from a verbal confrontation to a firefight, and on through military tactics. For example, imagine an interview subject becoming agitated while standing on a sidewalk. There is an advantageous position from where you can physically control the subject before the subject can touch you. This is difficult to visualize without a physical demonstration, but trust us, it's there. In this position you are safest, and the subject is also safe if the situation de-escalates and no physical control is necessary. You don't want a potentially compliant opponent to resist because you have not made it safe enough for him or her to surrender. Of course, finding the best tactical space is easier said than done. You need to train yourself to know what the safe space looks like and be able to see it while talking, surveying the surroundings, and evaluating the subject's dangerousness. Distractions won't disappear, but you need to see around and between them to find the safe space.

Think about a firefight. A position of cover from which we can return fire from relative safety is probably the safest spot. The goal is to see the path along which we can maneuver to the safest cover position while still being aware of the shooter, bystanders, and obstacles. The distractions in this case are even harder to ignore, but we can train ourselves to see between the distractions to find the safest place from which we can protect ourselves and others.

This is actually connected to our "mental toughness." Just as we can see between physical distractions to find the safest place to be, we can also "see" between emotional distractions to find the best mental outlook. Most sane people will never eliminate anger, fear, or excitement from their mind in a conflict, but those emotions do not use up all the capacity of your brain. The goal is to see the spaces between the emotions that will allow you to apply your physical training, tactical knowledge, and ethical clarity.

How do you train yourself to mentally see around and between the distractions of your emotions? The place to start is with tactical and protector mindset training. We offer both at Resolution Group International, but there are many credible programs throughout law enforcement academies and training companies across the country. The key is to be aware of the emotions, but not focus on them. Instead of trying not to feel emotions, accept them and look between and beyond them to compose a clearer mental picture. With practice, the mental and physical practice of seeing the space can become a unified skill.

Law enforcement officers are human beings often called on to do super-human things. Through insight, training, and experience, human emotions can either become an asset like courage, or a liability to be controlled like fear. The concept of seeing the space has infinite applications. Using this framework to sharpen mental focus under stress can have important practical benefits. Think about seeing the space the next time you are in a stressful situation. If you can find the spaces between and beyond the emotions, what do you see? You may just see a creative solution that saves lives. That is the Ethical Protector's number one job.

14

More Than the Sum of the Parts

Take water, hops, yeast, and malt. Stir it together in a glass. What you get is... well, it's not beer. Creating Ethical Protectors is not the same as brewing beer, obviously. Yet, it could be said that, although many departments provide a robust training curriculum—all of the ingredients of policing—it is not easy to "brew" a great officer or organizational culture.

Any attempt at conflict resolution by a law enforcement officer will always involve ethical, tactical, and technical elements. Training is used to prepare officers in each of these areas. However, most training focuses on each of these elements in isolation. The hope is providing all the right training "ingredients" will synergize within the officer, making him a motivated and skillful professional. Sometimes it happens. But experience has shown superior results may require more than just the right elements. Those elements must be introduced into the training in a certain way—that is, together. Ethics, tactics, and techniques, when they are all taught synergistically in a training setting, can have a lasting positive impact.

Basic law enforcement training necessarily focuses on the myriad technical aspects of the job. All the tools along the conflict resolution spectrum are taught, from ethics and laws to verbal communication to the use of firearms—and many subjects in between. Tactical training is introduced after a solid foundation of basic skills is established. Ethical training, which is usually weighted toward legal issues, is typically taught in an academic setting. One learns to shoot on the range, move tactically in a shoot-house, and behave ethically in a classroom. The time devoted to each of these areas follows the same order. The most time is devoted to technical training, less to individual and group tactics, and less still to ethics. This approach tends to reinforce a paradigm that resolves conflict by selecting a technique, adjusting the technique based on tactical considerations, and finally deciding whether the technique is legally permissible.

Most professionals agree, under the stress of conflict, one falls back on their training rather than rising to the occasion. It is here where the time and focus on technical training becomes the predominant reference point for reaction to conflict. Disaster can occur if the officer fails to also factor in the tactical and ethical considerations necessary for the protection of self and others. This disconnect between ethics, tactics and techniques can cause problems at all levels of activity, from a car stop to a major operation.

A famous 1985 incident in a major American city is particularly illustrative of the problem caused by disconnected ethics, tactics, and techniques. The police department was faced with one of the most dangerous situations in law enforcement: A group of armed and committed radical activists were refusing to vacate a fortified house. Weapons fire was being exchanged and efforts to penetrate the barricaded structure with tear gas canisters were ineffective. Faced with these critical circumstances, those in charge chose to employ a military technique in a law enforcement situation resulting in the most famous, and perhaps only, use of aerial bombardment in American law enforcement history. Two one-pound bombs of a dynamite substitute explosive were dropped from a helicopter onto the roof of the house. The intention was to breach the barricaded roof to introduce tear gas into the building. The resulting explosion and fire caused the deaths of eleven people—six adults and five children—and destroyed approximately sixty homes.

The political, legal, ethical, and personal ramifications of this action reverberated for years and continue to do so.

But for our purposes, the key point is that techniques and tactics were employed that were in direct conflict with the mission of justifiable law enforcement: *Protect your life and the life of others, all others, even the adversary, if possible.* The need to break a dangerous stalemate caused leaders to choose a technique with consequences that were not protective of life and property. The technique drove the tactics which led to the ethical failure.

An alternative model is to approach conflicts from the perspective of the Ethical Protector. A firm understanding of the Dual Life Value will lead to choosing appropriate tactics to ensure the protection of self and others and to the employment of the most effective techniques and technology. This model also requires a shift in training philosophy. To the greatest extent possible, ethics must be taught during tactical and technical training. This provides an integrated understanding of moral values in action, which is the definition of ethics.

How would that training look? Well, it might look quite different from the way it is usually conducted.

The Marine Corps Martial Arts Program is designed synergistically and consists of three main elements:

1. Character: Ethical training.
2. Mental: Military skills and protector mindset training.
3. Physical: Martial combatives and combat conditioning.

Notably, ethics training is the core of the program. We also have learned it is unproductive to teach ethics in the classroom. The Marines—and police officers—fall asleep! We now know that the best way to integrate ethics into the training is right in the middle of the physical training (tactical and/or technical). Train for a bit, get the juices flowing, and then interject moral value tie-ins like the Hunting Story and the Japanese Prisoner of War Story—

or appropriate stories of your own—smoothly into the mix.

There are many wonderful police officer stories that teach a moral lesson that can be used. During roll call, make your announcements, but then have everyone practice cuffing and uncuffing drills for two minutes; then have someone tell a short tie-in story. In other words, do the ethical, tactical, and technical training all together.

More formal tactical skills training, such as martial arts and defensive tactics training sessions, is even better opportunities to work the formula. Not only do they enhance officer survivability, but when conducted safely and properly, they can also be an excellent conditioning regimen—physically, mentally, and morally.

An important additional benefit is this kind of training is a sure-fire way to build camaraderie and an Ethical Protector *culture* within your organization. Anyone who has experienced shared adversity can attest to it as an activating ingredient for comradery and morale. Physical training sessions can also be one of the greatest time-savers and force-multipliers at the disposal of a creative leader. The reason is that the bonding that occurs following the physical training creates the perfect atmosphere for candid discussions. This is a great way to cover essential subjects, annual training requirements, value story tie-ins, and other important topics. It is a perfect time to discuss officer safety, alcohol abuse, sexual harassment, and even burn out. Why waste time moving people to a classroom? Hit them while they are open-minded and energized. It just works better.

15

Philosophy Drives Actions

Many things happen in the mind of a law enforcement officer when an encounter with a situation becomes violent. Training, judgment, and self-control compete with confusion, anger, and fear, so we must be careful how prime we our minds. The officer needs to instantly take the necessary actions to protect himself or herself and others—that's the job. The actions need to be effective, legal, and appropriate for the level of danger involved. And for many reasons—including the officer's own mental health—those actions must be ethical. In a world where the encounter will likely be captured on video, how can we develop a mindset to help us accomplish the mission and guard against legal and ethical problems?

The Ethical Protector mindset is an attitude of awareness, confidence, and purpose—awareness of the situation, confidence in our physical skills, and clarity of our legal and ethical purpose. Preparation for any critical moment requires a synergistic program of ethical, physical, and mental training. Let us, again, turn to the development of a protector mindset that produces fast and effective ethical action under the pressure of physical danger.

The Three Disciplines

To gain perspective, we will again use the U.S. Marine Corps Martial Arts Program (MCMAP) as a frame of reference. Marines involved in counterinsurgency operations are often placed in a role like a peace officer. They protect and serve the communities in their areas of operation, interact with a suspicious public, and do their best to build popular support for their work. When violence occurs, they are held accountable for using the appropriate amount of force along a defined continuum.

The Marines have found that the three disciplines of MCMAP—physical, mental, and ethical—help them act decisively in the right way at the right time. It helps them act in a way that keeps faith with the people they are protecting, helps them live with the consequences of their actions, and allows them to remain the most effective fighting force in the world.

The phrase "mind-body-spirit" is often associated with the martial arts. Many people assume that this is a philosophical concept requiring years of study and mystical initiation. The connection between mind, body, and spirit outlines a very accessible and practical system.

> **Mind:** The ability to organize and control one's thoughts.
> **Body:** Technical and tactical ability.

Spirit: The moral clarity that guides one's actions and are the building blocks of the protector mindset.

Whether it happens consciously or not, all physical actions begin in the mind. Even so-called "muscle memory" is just a faster version of the mind-body connection. The problem is even on a good day the mind is managing many things at once. The added stress of physical danger can turn multi-tasking into system overload. A well-developed protector mindset enables the quick effective thinking that triggers quick effective action. Again, what philosophical perspective are you priming your mind with?

Confidence in our physical skills can only come through effective training. Just as MCMAP is designed for military combat, there are many combative systems geared toward law enforcement. A system useful for developing the protector mindset should have some specific characteristics:

THE ETHICAL PROTECTOR

1. The system should be based on sound tactical principles as much as fighting techniques.

2. It should employ techniques that are simple to learn, easy to practice and adaptable to many conflict situations.

3. It should focus on keeping the officer's weapon safe — and available, if needed.

The goal is to develop a set of quickly deployable physical tools that can be used in a variety of dangerous situations.

Underlying these tactical and technical considerations is the spirit of the Ethical Protector which serves to clarify our purpose. The protector protects him or herself and others. The others can be a partner, a bystander, or even the suspect. When a situation turns violent, this spirit and commitment to protect life forms the foundation of our purpose. This clarity provides reassurance that our use of physical force is justified, allowing us to act decisively with the confidence that we will not regret our actions.

The goal of developing a protector mindset is to do the right thing, in the right way, for the right reason, all under extreme stress. Physical training and ethical clarity support a mindset that identifies and deals with danger in an effective and dispassionate way. Every officer knows that a quiet shift can instantly turn into the ultimate test. Developing a professional protector mindset can be an important tool for excelling at that test.

16

Ethics Drive Tactics; Tactics Drive Technique

At Resolution Group International we have a saying: Ethics drive tactics, tactics drive technique. Being ethical and even employing great tactics might not be enough to preclude the need to use physical techniques in some situations. We are lifetime martial artists: Jack is a Subject Matter Expert for the Marine Corps Martial Arts Program and Bruce is certified as both a firearms and general police instructor. We know it can get downright physical. However, please consider how you would answer the following question.

We were recently approached by a defensive tactics instructor from a major police department who requested our opinion regarding the Vascular Neck Restraint (VNR).

This instructor has 30 years of martial arts training and 25 years as a police officer and he was concerned about the "muddy" prospect of training officers to use this type of technique.

We agree with his assessment of the training—it can be muddy. The VNR is a highly effective technique. But, if improperly applied, it can have disastrous results.

Before any technique is used, some conditions must be satisfied:

1. Is it ethical? Do my intended actions protect myself and others—even my suspect, if possible?

2. Is it tactical? Does the specific environment and atmosphere of the situation require a strong physical response?

3. Is the physical response technically appropriate? Does my intended

action (technique) — in context —
satisfy #1 and #2.

4. Am I competent to take that action (perform that technique) without losing my clarity of mind (my protector mindset)?

In other words, will using this technique, at this time and place, protect self and others? Or am I using it out of fear, anger, disrespect, as a punishment, or to protect my ego? Using a technique, any technique, without satisfying #1 and #2 — or even discussing it beforehand — is, indeed, a recipe for "muddiness." Muddiness can lead to possibly an inappropriate and perhaps even illegal outcome.

In most Defensive Tactics courses, officers are likely to get good technical instruction on the technique at hand. Officers will also probably hear the legal ramifications of using the technique. However, it is also critical that they review:

I. The imperative considerations for ethical application:

1. Am I making myself disproportionately safer at the suspect's expense—will they die?
2. Might *I* die if I don't employ this technique.
3. Is this potentially lethal technique necessary to protect myself and others?

II. Necessity for maintaining a clear protector mindset:

1. Am I capable of controlling my anger and fear enough to apply the technique effectively and dispassionately?
2. Can I maintain the awareness to recognize compliance and switch to a different control technique if possible?

III. Importance of being acutely aware of the tactical appropriateness:

1. Am I using this technique because it "works," or because it is the most appropriate response in the situation?
2. Am I making myself vulnerable to other attackers by "locking on" to the suspect?

If all those considerations are addressed, then officers will know that whatever techniques they are taught will likely be used appropriately. We do not pretend officers have the time to review these considerations under the stress and danger of an actual physical conflict situation. We believe they must be clarified *beforehand*. The first time you think these things through should not be when you are preparing to defend your actions in court. A sustained program of realistic physical training fully incorporating tactics and ethics gives officers the best chance to be prepared and to do the right thing.

As far as the VNR goes, it has gone out of favor because the technique has been applied incorrectly too many times. It was sometimes used without the proper ethical and tactical considerations. This is a shame because it can be a useful and effective technique. But it is amoral. Criminals can use the VNR too, by the way. Even if your agency's policy allows it, please use it as an Ethical Protector.

17

Martial Skills

Some folks have a terribly difficult time taking the right action under duress. The answer why is simple: They are philosophically confused, emotionally overwhelmed, and subject to being afraid, embarrassed, or prone to freeze under stress. So, what can we do to help others gain the ability to, "do the right thing," even under great adversity? There may not be one answer that works for everyone, but there appears to be a formula that works for most people:

Moral + Physical = Ethical.

1. People benefit from a clarification of their beliefs and a practical

understanding of how values, morals, and ethics work.

2. Physical confidence bolsters moral courage. When you possess physical skills, it is easier to act ethically, even if it never "gets physical."

When you break it down like this, a methodology for developing Ethical Protectors becomes clearer. Consider a training formula that combines philosophical clarification with martial arts training. You may end up with a wonderful contingent of Ethical Protectors in your organization.

There is also some confusion about "sport martial arts" vs. "defensive tactics" or "combatives." This topic bears some examination. There are certainly some similarities between sport martial arts and combatives. There is striking and grappling in both, of course. And good boxers, wrestlers and jujitsu practitioners certainly have an advantage in the street compared to the untrained. But there are a number of important differences between sports and fighting in the street.

First, the emotional piece. Certainly, a sport fight can be exciting and stressful, but it doesn't compare to fighting for one's life.

And the "tunnel vision" that comes with adrenalized activity is really not so dangerous in the ring. The referee is there to make sure nothing gets out of hand, even if the competitors get caught up in the experience and over focus.

And then there is the real-world tactical environment. There is no soft mat, there is no safety gear, weapons might be involved, or even multiple attackers. None of those things are a danger in the ring.

But the most important difference, as it pertains to the Ethical Protector, may be philosophical. When people fight for sport, they fight for themselves—perhaps to exercise their natural competitive urges or to win a trophy. There is really nothing wrong with sport fighting. We are not against martial sports, as long as they don't get too violent or make the participants too selfish.

Many people also think of martial arts in terms of "self-defense." Certainly, self-defense is ethical and martial arts skill can be used to protect the self. Yet, anyone would protect themselves if they could. That does not necessarily make them a protector—or ethical, for that matter.

Ethical Protectors don't fight only for themselves; they fight for their communities, their families, and friends—they fight for others. And this often comes at the risk of the protector's own safety—perhaps his or her own life. This is a profound and fundamental philosophical difference between sport combatives and the protector's martial skills.

18

Defensive Tactics Training

As the Bully Story (Chapter Five) illustrates, ethics are ultimately moral-physical. Moral people may want to step up and do the right thing, but they often lack the physical courage and ability. Martial arts can provide the necessary skills and confidence. That is why Ethical Protector training includes—and must include—martial arts, especially for professionals like Marines or LEOs.

It is also important that the training be ongoing. An interesting challenge with Ethical Protector training is that the lessons tend to "wear off" without sustainment. The Protector Ethic must be maintained by continuous moral-physical training. For the Marines, that means at least a few hours a week of the physical

MCMAP training with the value tie-ins. For law enforcement, that would mean a deliberate effort to integrate appropriate Protector Ethic tie-ins into some type of tactical training.

People are attracted to the law enforcement profession for many reasons. Most are motivated by a desire to make a positive difference by protecting and serving their communities. Many are also attracted to the prestige, authority, and respect that come with the profession. They may also want to be part of a close-knit team with high standards and *esprit de corps*. Some want to stand out among their fellow citizens for accepting sacrifices and facing dangers. Still others may just want, for lack of a better word, a "cool" job.

We hope all law enforcement professionals start out wanting to be Ethical Protectors, even if they don't use that term specifically. But all too often, after a few years on the job, there is a transformation, and not always a good one. The original motivations are still there beneath the surface, but the complexities of the real world may lead to a world-weary cynicism. What about the prestige, respect, and authority we thought we would acquire? The bond of service with brother and sister officers becomes the primary source of motivation and pride. Distance grows between the officers ("us") and the people for whom we joined law enforcement and swore to protect ("them").

Cynicism affects more than just our behavior on the street, it can also affect our approach to training, especially defensive tactics training. We believe defensive tactics training is an ideal setting for clarifying and refining the ethical values that keep officers safe and effective. All organizations are different, and you might not identify with the scenario described below, but many will probably see some distinct similarities with their training experiences.

A typical day of defensive tactics refresher training begins with the officer-students less than enthused. There is probably some nervous joking and laughter, maybe driven by the fear of somehow getting embarrassed or hurt. Most are probably not particularly interested in martial arts and think they already know everything they need to know. Their street experiences didn't look like the simple role-playing scenes that they were taught in the academy gym anyway.

The instructor appears before this less-than-receptive audience. Not immune from cynicism, the instructor adds his or her own professional baggage to the atmosphere. There is the temptation to make a big impression to gain the attention of an unenthusiastic class. Often this impression is a display of toughness, physical strength, or technical skill. The physical display can be accompanied by a verbal show of toughness. Toughness can quickly turn into meanness. The emphasis is on damage to the opponent, and restraint is only discussed in terms of legal liability.

If the instructor insists on physically demanding training, the officer-students are likely to either hang back to prevent injury or display excessive aggression to mirror the instructor's attitude. If, on the other hand, the instructor is concerned that the audience resents the training, physical demands may become lighter and the training less effective. Either way, no one is likely to leave with a positive experience. None experience the noble feeling of being an Ethical Protector. What can be done?

Train to Protect Others

Try building the others-protecting message right into the training. Practice the physical techniques not only in defense of self, but also in defense of others. In our combined five decades of martial arts training, we have been in literally hundreds of martial arts schools and defensive tactics sessions and we have seen thousands of techniques. Reliably, 99% of these techniques involve the person protecting themselves. But how about some training in protecting others? We have found that training to protect others heightens enthusiasm and motivation and suppresses unproductive competitive urges. Some of us have done personal protection work and we know that learning to protect others can make a positive improvement in the psychological atmosphere of the training.

For those who may be interested in learning and teaching the others-protecting techniques, the approach is simple. Use the same techniques you already know but set up scenarios in which multiple people are attacking a person you are protecting. It is interesting, fun, and you can learn a lot about the technicalities of real-life protective actions.

Try these scenarios. Be creative and make up your own.

Scenario 1

You and your partner are interviewing a subject. The subject suddenly takes a wild swing at your partner or goes for his or her weapon. Can you protect your partner, keep yourself and your weapon tactically safe, and subdue the subject with just the right level of force?

Scenario 2
You and a partner are breaking up a shoving match between two subjects. Can you effectively maneuver in a way that separates them and lets your partner restrain one person while you restrain the other?

Here is a guideline that may help you remain true to the Ethical Protector mindset: The object is not to fight the "bad guy," rather, focus on protecting everyone involved. It is a subtle difference, but it can make all the difference.

19

Police "Militarization"

Is American law enforcement becoming an overly aggressive commando army? Are our police becoming militarized, adopting the weapons and attitudes of the battlefield for policing America's streets? Allegations that law enforcement has been militarized are a popular topic in the media—people are even writing books about it. Is this concern valid? Do military styled tactical teams make routine law enforcement more dangerous to the public? Wouldn't we all be safer if LEOs acted more like Andy Griffith than Rambo?

We don't define "warrior" merely as "one who engages in war." That definition lumps together mercenaries and terrorists with U.S. Marines and legitimate freedom fighters. We define a warrior as a protector of life: ourselves, the innocent and even our enemies, when possible. An Ethical Protector's mission is to protect every life possible and to use force only when it's necessary to accomplish that mission.

Does the life-protecting definition of an Ethical Protector include the sub-machine gun wielding cop dressed head-to-toe in body armor? We think it can. Properly equipped, trained, and led, this LEO is more likely to keep self and others safe in a dangerous situation. Why? Simple: Conflict is not a sport. Fair fights are dangerous. Fairness may be a basic human value—a common American value—but it is a relative value. It must be qualified as good or bad and "good to whom" based upon its contribution to protecting life.

The reality is that fairness can be deadly under the right circumstances. Fair fights are dangerous because both sides have a reasonable chance to win, and they last longer because the sides are evenly matched. We question people's courage when they quit a fair fight, but we tend to forgive surrender against overwhelming odds.

There are too many variables in a dynamic conflict situation to keep a fair fight safe. Since the good guys have to win, there has to be a healthy margin of error.

For example, during the arrest of a possibly violent subject the last thing we want is a fair fight. We want the arrest to be lawful, safe, and respectful of the subject's civil rights. We don't want to give the subject the impression that escape through violent resistance might be successful. We want the subject to instantly recognize that resistance is futile and surrender peacefully.

A well-trained and equipped tactical team makes everyone in the arrest situation safer. The officers are safer because they are executing a frequently rehearsed scenario. Bystanders are safer because, should deadly force be necessary, the team is likely to only hit what they are shooting at (tactical weapons may appear more dangerous, but they are actually safer because they are very precise). Finally, the subject is safer because resistance is less likely.

No situation is free of possible problems. Although a well-trained tactical team is safer, there may be temptations to overuse the team in situations the public may not perceive to be appropriate. More concerning is the possibility that tactical operators will start to view themselves as warfighters up against an enemy force, instead of officers enforcing the law and protecting their communities. This temptation makes it vitally important for tactical operators to activate, clarify, and sustain the life-protecting Ethical Protector mindset.

It comes down to training, leadership and, yes, ethics. Just putting on a bunch of tactical gear (or getting in a surplus tank—yes, tank!), does not mean you are an Ethical Protector making communities safer. That kind of gear demands commensurate technical, tactical, and philosophical excellence.

Technology can't drive tactics. As the saying goes: When all you have is a hammer, everything starts to look like a nail. Remember, ethics drive tactics which drives the use of technology—not the other way around. Additionally, we must ask ourselves this question: If we are not trained to use the equipment, should we really be employing it in a real conflict situation?

Ethics drive tactics; tactics drive technique.

One point worth considering is that for years our military has been evolving counterinsurgency (COIN) operations that are far less militarized than those employed in the past. COIN has the goal of winning the hearts and minds of the people in our areas of operation. Creating mutually respectful relationships facilitates cooperation and collaboration between our forces and the locals to root out enemy insurgents. This approach requires respect, hard work, and looks a lot more like community policing than an assault on Iwo Jima's Mount Suribachi.

The Ethical Protector

While Rambo may not be a great role model for today's law enforcement officer, the public has nothing to fear from well-trained tactical teams made up of motivated Ethical Protectors.

20

Take a Break and Tell a Story

People love great stories. We have recounted several Ethical Protector stories in these pages. These types of stories clarify our purpose and remind us with emotional impact of why we wanted to be protectors in the first place.

The intense physical nature and shared adversity of tactical training is the perfect environment to share protector stories. Nothing motivates the troops more, at end of a tough day of training, than hearing stories that help clarify, activate, and sustain the protector ethic.

How else can we bridge the gap between instructor and the instructed, and create the conditions for meaningful training—and mutual learning? We suggest that the rest break immediately after physical training is a perfect opportunity to reconnect with those ethical motivations that originally brought everyone to law enforcement. Overcoming the embarrassment and discomfort of physical contact can break down cynicism and the reluctance to discuss the real purpose of the job.

When we activate the idea that our tactical and technical skills serve to protect ourselves and others, all others if possible, we begin to reconnect to our ethical roots. If you are worried about being embarrassed, don't be. Think about our leadership advice; act as if everyone else will value the discussion. So, talk about why you want to be in law enforcement in a very natural way after the training. Use real life protector stories with emotional impact to activate the feeling of being a protector. We all have these anecdotes, so share them! It helps us regain the view of ourselves as Ethical Protectors. And that, if you think about it, is a cool job.

21

The Warrior Creed

The Warrior Creed was expressed by the late Dr. Robert Humphrey. It offers concrete guidance for developing the habits of an Ethical Protector in our daily lives.

As a young Marine Captain, just off the drill field at the Recruit Depot in San Diego, Jack decided to earn his master's degree at night. That is where he met his mentor, Robert Humphrey—he was one of Jack's professors.

Bob Humphrey was a child of the Great Depression. Those were the days when life's lessons were learned in the school of hard knocks and he earned money as a semi-professional boxer. He also rode freight trains, worked in the Civilian Conservation Corps (the CCCs), and finally joined the Merchant

Marines. He transferred to the U.S. Marine Corps during World War II and became a rifle-platoon leader on Iwo Jima, receiving a gunshot wound that ended his hopes for a professional boxing career. After he was honorably discharged from the Marines, he earned a degree at Harvard Law school and settled into teaching Economics at MIT.

During the Cold War, he went back overseas to see if his worldly experiences and Ivy League education would guide him in solving America's cross-cultural relations issues. Too often these issues were exacerbated by America's own self-defeating and arrogant "Ugly Americanism." This is well documented in his experiences in Asia Minor and chronicled in the Hunting Story.

Jack recalls:

Bob was a hell of a man and a real warrior, as opposed to me, who at the time just thought I was. To tell the truth, I thought I was a "tough-guy." I would walk around town with a scowl on my face, challenging everyone I met with my eyes. Have you ever fantasized about using your martial arts training? That was me. I would walk into a bar or restaurant, look the place over, and then mentally kill everyone before I could relax, sit down, and have a beer.

My aggressive attitude started to irritate Humphrey to the point that he finally took me aside and said, "Jack, do you realize you make people uncomfortable? You have a way of challenging everyone you meet."

I shrugged. But inside I was secretly pleased; they *should* be uncomfortable—I'm Marine *and* a martial artist!

Humphrey could see I wasn't getting it. But he was patient and smart. Rather than telling me I was a fool, he gave me some extra homework, "Jack, tonight when you go out, instead of looking at everyone like you want to intimidate them, try this instead. Say to yourself, 'everyone in this place is a little safer because I am here.'"

The Ethical Protector

I respected Humphrey very much by this time, so I decided to try his suggestion. I often went to a place in Ocean Beach called the Red Garter. It was like the cantina from "Star Wars"—full of tough-guys (and gals), various military members, bikers, even Soviet spies (this was during the Cold War!). Anyway, there was plenty of trouble if you wanted it.

But this time, instead of acting like my usual self, I stopped in the doorway, surveyed the scene and said silently: "Everyone in this place is a little safer because I am here. Anyone in need has at least one friend because of me and my skills."

Well, everybody ignored me, of course, nothing happened on the outside. But on the inside, I felt a remarkable change. It was an epiphany. And it changed my life. Even as I write this, I get that same tingly feeling on my face and scalp I had then. I realized, "Wow! That felt a lot better than whatever I was doing!"

That lesson in context changed my life and possibly even saved it. It turned me from a self-styled "badass" into a protector and I continue to recommend it all over the world. I invite you to try it yourself.

The Warrior Creed

Wherever I go,
everyone is a little bit safer because I am there.

Wherever I am,
anyone in need has a friend.

When I return home,
everyone is happy I am there.

It's a better life!

The Creed can work as well on the street as it does in a bar. The Ethical Protector should be so confident in his or her skills that overt intimidation becomes unnecessary. The classic police motto, "to protect and serve," is perfectly aligned with the idea that everyone is safer because we are there.

22

A True Test of the Warrior Creed

Becoming an Ethical Protector can enhance a law enforcement officer's effectiveness at work, but it can also improve the quality of life at home. We often judge success by our accomplishments on the job, but how would we stack-up if success were measured by our accomplishments at home? The great LEO with a train-wreck family life is a common stereotype, but one all too often based on reality.

Even today, when we walk through the mall, sit in the subway, or pass through the scary part of town, we sometimes wonder if we are confident and secure enough in our values and skills to live the admonition of the Warrior Creed. Can we project an acknowledgment of human equality into the eyes of everyone we meet? Even people who may have behaviors we don't particularly like or agree with—perhaps even criminal behaviors? Can we separate the relative value of their behavior, which may be good, bad, or indifferent, from the universal, intrinsic value of their life, and remain the protector? Is everyone in our presence truly safer because we are there?

Jack has shared the story of his Red Garter epiphany regarding warrior and protector ethics with audiences all over the world. The vast majority of them feel living life as an Ethical Protector is a "better life." Yet...

Jack relates:

One of the byproducts of telling the Warrior Creed story is that people sometimes view me as an "enlightened warrior," but that does not mean I am. I did enjoy the accolades, though. At one point I even began to think they were my due for bringing Humphrey's powerful message to the world. But here's a little secret: It is not that difficult to look like a big deal for a few hours or even days in front of a sympathetic group. The real test is at home. Almost exactly 16 years after that homework assignment at the bar, I learned I was not yet the Ethical Protector I thought I was.

Dr. Humphrey was visiting my home. We were doing a seminar that combined warrior ethics and combative skills in one moral-physical lesson. That would be the next day. But it was Friday, and I was still working my day job up in North Jersey, nearly a 60-mile commute from my house. It was March—sleeting—and traffic was horrible. I had already had a bad day at work. I couldn't wait to get out of there and it took me about two-and-a-half hours to get home on the icy roads. I got out of the car and walked up to my front door and just about had smoke coming out of my ears. Ever had a day like that?

Imagine this scene as I opened the door and walked into my house: Dr. Humphrey was sitting on the couch in the living room with my two kids crawling all over him, laughing, and playing. My wife was in the kitchen cooking and singing. And I'm standing there after having this horrible day and for some reason the whole scene just made me angry! I thought to myself, "I'm glad everyone is having such a great time while I am driving home in a sleet storm bringing home the bacon!" Dr. Humphrey glanced up at me from the couch, took one look at my face and said, "Get out!"

Get out? I said, "Wait a minute, this is my house." Again, he said, "Get out!"

So, I got out.

I walked outside and stood under our little covered porch in the sleet. Dr. Humphrey came out and looked at me—sternly at first, then kindly. He said softly, "Jack, do you know what was going on in this house before you walked into this house? Everybody was waiting in joyous anticipation. We couldn't wait for you to get home, because we were all going to have dinner and be together and enjoy the evening. And you walked in the door looking like that.

In three seconds, you broke the heart of everyone in this house. Is that what you were trying to do, Mr. "Ethical Warrior?"

I was ashamed. I felt about an inch tall.

He went on, "If you're really going to be a warrior, these are the people you need to protect—especially their feelings and their hearts."

This is where the last component of "The Warrior Creed" came from, "When I return home, everyone is happy I am there. It's a better life!"

The challenge is to always remember to protect our loved ones. There is an old saying: "You always hurt the ones you love." We know that after a difficult tour—or even a tough day at the office—it is common to bring the stress and fear home with us. But the Ethical Protector recognizes that the work is not done when we come "home from the wars."

Rather, our most important job is just starting. That is, to protect and defend the ones we love the most. So, try on the Warrior Creed for size. Living by this simple admonition may take us a long way toward decreasing officer burnout and the all too common domestic problems. In many ways, living the last part of the creed is the most difficult. But if we can, it truly is a better life.

23

PRESILIENCY:
Combating PTSD and Moral Injury

Research has shown that dehumanizing criminal suspects aggravates stress and harms the law enforcement officer (LEO) involved. Can training in specialized ethics help LEOs to avoid the trap of dehumanization? Can officers be "immunized" against the damage of Post-Traumatic Stress Disorder (PTSD) and moral injury? We believe so.

A new term, "presiliency" (prē-ˈzil-yən(t)-sē) is offered to describe training that seeks to strengthen LEOs philosophically, psychologically, and physically before they are subjected to the stresses of their duties. Dealing with that stress after the fact is too late. Presiliency training re-calibrates the moral compass with an ethical "true north" combined with mental toughness instruction and intense physical drilling, to develop an ethical protector mindset. The Marine Corps' successes with such training will be highlighted.

PTSD and Moral Injury

The terms "PTSD" and "moral injury" are often used interchangeably, but they are distinct and should not be confused:

Post-traumatic stress is *inflicted upon* someone by outside events and circumstances.

Moral injury is *self-inflicted*.

Deep emotional reactions are virtually unavoidable for those involved in stressful and dangerous situations, particularly those that are a matter of a traumatic, life and death nature. There is sufficient psychological evidence to state life or death combat and killing is so abhorrent to normal humans, that it is inherently damaging to virtually everyone who participates. In fact, it could be said it would be *unnatural* if people did not get some degree of PTSD from such traumatic exposure. There is a wealth of research on the how and why of PTSD that need not be reiterated here. But the main point is this: PTSD is inflicted *upon* those involved in circumstances of war, combat, and other traumatic events, and it is virtually unavoidable.

Moral injury is different. If PTSD is something that is inflicted upon a person from the outside, then moral injury is inflicted from within. Moral injury can occur when, under the stresses of traumatic circumstances, a person performs an act which he or she later profoundly regrets. They feel ashamed and/or embarrassed about an action they would not have even considered without the extreme stress. These actions often involve dehumanization and can be manifested in maltreatment, abuse, and even murder.

Psychologically, at least two forms of PTSD may exist. In some cases, a healthy balanced regard for self and others gets knocked off kilter toward the self (Figure 1). Exposure to extreme danger and stress makes the sufferer act overly suspicious of others or "paranoid." Long after the traumatic event, when sufferers are safe at home, *everybody* may seem like an enemy, including friends and family.

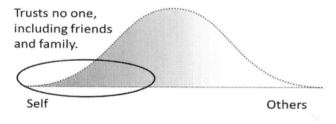

Figure 1

The others-protecting side of their human nature has been totally obscured by their pathology. We hear of severe PTSD cases in which sufferers trust no one, to the point that they will even attack or kill their spouses and children. The sufferer is alienated from others and hyper-focused on survival. But their "selfishness" brings no peace or happiness. Once a person gets this far off balance, as in any severe loss of stability, regaining a healthy equilibrium is very difficult.

Another form of PTSD manifests as a feeling of worthlessness (Figure 2).

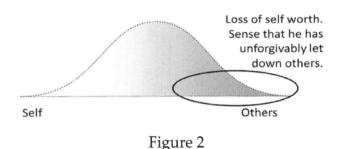

Figure 2

People with this form feel they should have done more to protect their partners or comrades, or they are filled with self-loathing for actions they took or failed to take. They may also feel intense guilt for killing or the loss of life. If they have dehumanized people, that will only deepen the problem.

Presiliency Training

The mission of law enforcement places officers at psychological risk. This is most evident during violent conflicts, but the constant potential for such conflicts also takes a toll. Law enforcement may need to kill or injure in defense of life. Killing another human being is inherently damaging, regardless of the necessity. Addressing post-traumatic stress after the fact is too little, too late.

We propose the new term "presiliency" to describe training that seeks to strengthen officers philosophically, psychologically, and physically *beforehand*. Much like prehabilitation, a form of strength training that is designed to prevent physical injuries before the actual occurrence, presiliency, is an enhanced state of ethical clarity and mental-physical toughness that reduces the risk of moral injury and PTSD under stress.

JACK E. HOBAN AND BRUCE J. GOURLIE

The last two decades of continuous conflict forced the U.S. Marine Corps to develop training designed to equip Marines to handle traumatic stress. We recognize the ongoing national debate about police "militarization." We fully recognize the important differences between military and police operations. But the traumatic stress associated with violence is a real human commonality which may benefit from a common solution. The Marine Corps Martial Arts Program (MCMAP) is a combination of clarified ethics, effective combative training, and mental toughness experiences. Marines practice under adverse conditions to overcome ineffective behavior under stress. Counterproductive emotion-based actions are "trumped" by learned moral-physical drilled responses. This ethics-based methodology has been effective in helping our warriors "do the right thing"—ethically, tactically and technically—both in combat and back in garrison.

It also proves itself useful in building

presiliency. We believe that "Ethical Warrior" training can address the dangers of combat stress, as well as the physical and psychological challenges faced by our wounded warriors. In other words, our experience is proving that such a training regimen can inoculate Marines—and, we believe, LEOs—from the stress of combat and physical violence and mediate the effects of PTSD afterward.

Presiliency training consists of (figure 3):

Figure 3

Ethical Clarification

Ethical clarification seeks to "calibrate the moral compass" by re-activating a deep seated and inherent conviction: that life is an objective and "absolute" value. As such it is an inalienable right shared by all people, and therefore, "all men (and women) are created equal." This "Life Value" is the "magnetic north" of the moral compass and the supporting premise of a Marine's other moral values, including the USMC core values of honor, courage, and commitment—none of which could be properly invoked as a virtue without first anchoring them to respect for the value of life.

Clarification of the Life Value is vital for presiliency because it safeguards our humanity and sets us apart from immoral people who do not respect the lives of others outside of their "in group."

For example, Marines are taught to respect the enemy's life, yet, to recognize—with guidance from the specific Rules of Engagement and the Laws of War—when the enemy's behavior is life-threatening to fellow Marines and/or other people within their area of responsibility. The Marine knows more clearly when the life-threatening behavior must be halted by capturing or killing the enemy. In other words: *Marines are trained to kill to protect life*.

This is most clear when observing the difference in how enemy wounded are treated. When combatants are wounded and no longer a threat, Marines render medical care. Conversely, if many of our enemies come upon a wounded Marine or vulnerable soldiers, they will invariably "finish them off."

By clarifying the magnetic north of the moral compass, the Ethical Warrior orients under the stress of combat by using the Life Value as the supporting premise of his or her other moral values (Figure 4).

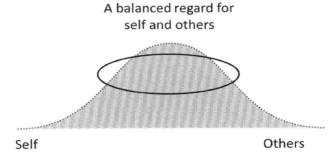

Figure 4

If the Life Value is not clarified, activated, and reinforced beforehand it may result in ethical confusion, manifesting in poor decision making, perhaps even causing a deadly "freeze" at a critical time. Worse, it can result in regarding others as "objects," and treating their life as a "relative" value—worth more or less based upon the individual's or group's behavior. This perspective, in turn, may lead to unlawful incidents in law enforcement, and in war, atrocities.

Mental Toughening

In order to accomplish the mission under the stress of combat, Marines receive relevant professional education, including "scenario-based" training. Military skills, however, are most reliably executed when Marine possess mental toughness. The term mental toughness (sometimes referred as a "Combat Mindset" or a "Protector Mindset") can be described as the ability to "do the right thing" under extreme emotional, psychological, and physical adversity or stress. This includes the ability to override the emotions, including the fight, freeze or flight mechanism, and act rationally to accomplish the mission in accordance with one's moral and physical training.

Counterproductive, purely emotion-based thoughts and actions are "trumped" by moral-physical responses. Being exposed to value "tie-ins," stories with emotional impact, allow Marines to feel the nobility of moral behavior in their "guts." Ethical leadership and physical training are also invaluable for building mental toughness and, ultimately, presiliency. Hard, realistic training under adversity is also an important ingredient for building Marine team cohesion through shared adversity.

Physical Training

With regard to presiliency training, three further elements are necessary:

- Martial Arts
- Combat Conditioning
- Shared Adversity

Physical toughness and conditioning support mental toughness and vice versa—the two go hand in hand. Martial arts training provides confidence and tangible self and others protection skills along the entire continuum of violence. Yet any training should be, at its core, an ethics-based program. Ethics creates protectors, and protectors are ethical — the two go hand in hand. The Marine Corps' MCMAP training is a moral character-based approach and quite different than any program based upon mere fighting skills that may or may not be directed toward the defense of others.

Summary

Doctors utilize "prehabilitation" to improve the functional capability of a patient prior to a surgical procedure, so the patient can withstand postoperative inactivity and associated decline. The goal is to get to a prepare physically *before* an operation to lessen the complications afterward.

If entering a burning building one would wear fire-retardant clothing, not go in unprotected and just plan to treat the burns afterward.

"Presiliency" is a term we use to describe training that strengthens LEOs philosophically, psychologically, and physically *before* being subjected to the stresses of violence and criminality. This gets a person to a better place ethically, mentally, and psychologically to reduce the possibility of developing PTSD. Dealing with post-traumatic stress after the fact is too late.

Presiliency training starts by ethically re-calibrating the moral compass with the absolute value of *life* as true north. This is followed by training that builds mental toughness and develops a protector mindset. The training has to be tough, realistic, and physical. A program like MCMAP is an ideal model for law enforcement to develop this kind of training. It is character-based and teaches effective life-protecting skills.

Ethics drive tactical choices, which in turn drive the specific techniques a LEO will actually use in defense of life. Clarifying those ethics beforehand, and drilling their physical responses to stress, can result in better trained, thus better prepared, and resilient law enforcement officers.

24

Training Camden:
Creating A Protector Culture

It is fair to ask if our writing, speaking, and training has had any lasting impact. Hundreds of LEOs have been through our basic Ethical Protector Course. While we have scores of positive testimonials from our students, we usually train only a few officers in each of many different organizations. Our influence has been more wide than deep. But there are several departments that have been different. One case in particular bears relating.

We were both involved in a large training program several years ago that tested our theories in, what was at the time, the most dangerous city in America. It was a unique opportunity. We were tasked with helping shape the culture and skills of the new Camden County Police Department (CCPD), virtually from scratch. The previous city police department had been disbanded due to an inability to control the high crime rate, poor relations with the community, and cost overruns.

The new Chief, Scott Thomson, heard Jack speak at a law enforcement leadership symposium at Stockton University and introduced himself. Months later Jack got a surprise call from the Chief's office asking him to come in and discuss how the "Ethical Protector" program, conducted by our company, Resolution Group International (RGI), could lead the training of the new department. The goal was to make the officers in this "start-up" department (1) ethical, (2) effective at verbal conflict resolution, and (3) tactically proficient in that particularly challenging environment.[4]

---

[4]https://www.nj.com/camden/index.ssf/2015/07/retired_us_marine_to_teach_camden_county_police_de.html

Over the many months we were there, we trained all the officers in tactics, de-escalation skills, and community policing methodologies, some adapted from the Marines' effective "winning hearts and mind" efforts overseas. At the core of the training was respect—respect for the sanctity of life. Whose life? Self and others. Which others? All others—including the criminals', if possible. Wherever our officers went, everyone would be safer because they were there. That ethic—of a life-protector—drove the new tactical philosophy and communication techniques. "Ethics drives tactics, tactics drive techniques," was the motto.

It seemed to work. Crime began to drop, community engagement increased, and officer morale rose. CCPD started to get cautious, but optimistic, press coverage.

After fading from the scene, we were anxious to see if the new training philosophies and methodologies would stick. Could CCPD sustain the transition? Would the lives of the officers and citizens of Camden continue to improve? Or would the culture revert to the bad old days of out-of-control crime and poor community relations?

We are happy to see that the culture has remained true to the Ethical Protector (or Guardian, as they now call it) culture. Today, Camden is often cited in the news as a model of effective community policing[5], and crime is way down.[6] Making the officers think of themselves as "protectors," along with deploying new de-escalation tactics, saved a life almost right away.[7]

The credit, of course, rightfully goes to the men and women of the Camden County Police Department who created and maintained the new culture and to their courageous and visionary leadership. Bruce and Jack's direct

---

[5]https://www.gloucestercitynews.net/clearysnotebook/2017/10/camden-county-police-departmenta-model-for-community-connection.html

[6] (https://www.citylab.com/equity/2018/01/what-happened-to-crime-in-camden/549542/

[7]https://www.nj.com/opinion/index.ssf/2017/04/camden_county_cops_changing_the_culture_editorial.html. Video here: https://www.youtube.com/watch?v=YtVUMT9P8iw

roles have ended for now. However, we think it might be helpful for others who are intrigued by the dramatic transformation in Camden to know about the unique methodology that was used to initiate the change. We were intimately involved with that.

We did several "out of the box" things that appeared to work you might try. Here they are:

1. **Top-down support, buy-in at all levels, participation by all.** It was Chief Thomson who made a 100% commitment to the new program. Granted, he was able to start with a fairly "clean slate," as the new CCPD had a fresh start with many new, young officers. But there is no way you can create a new culture (or change one) without everyone, particularly the leadership, being fully engaged. Chief Thomson started by getting all the leadership together, introducing Jack and RGI and emphasizing that the Ethical Protector culture would be the Number 1 priority in the Department. Then we scheduled "port and starboard" training for the

entire Department where we gave every single officer a one-hour overview of the new Program. Then it was mandated that everyone get thoroughly trained—including the Captains and Deputy Chiefs. Everyone. Often police leadership tries to introduce a new program, but the actual training gets foisted on the rank and file while the leadership remains in their offices. Camden didn't do that.

2. **Create a Mentor Cadre.** Concurrent with the Program overview training, we asked Chief Thomson to select his 20 most respected and charismatic officers—not the most highly ranked, necessarily, but the ones most looked up to by their peers. His first choice was the training officer. A former Marine and a "walk-on-water" field cop. Together we selected the next 19. Some were lieutenants, some were sergeants, but many were patrol officers, several with overseas combat experience. They came in all flavors—genders, races, job descriptions. They were given two

special "mentor courses" and we held bi-monthly mentor meetings to practice the new de-escalation and tactical skills. But most importantly we told stories. We talked about our own mentors and how they had impacted our lives. Stories of respectful behavior and heroism that we had witnessed were shared. And we celebrated them. In addition to setting the example for all officers and being available 24-7, they selected certain individuals in the Department who they felt connected to and could "take under their wing." Especially, we talked about officers who needed particular guidance, and we made sure someone would willingly mentor that person. By the way, we are not fans of traditional "train-the-trainer" programs. No matter how "vital" the information being passed, the idea that a few days (or hours!) of training qualifies a person to teach others, much less make the lessons stick, is mostly delusional. People need mentorship and sustainment to learn something, especially if the goal is to create a whole new positive attitude about their job.

The next step was having the mentors assist the RGI staff in teaching a three-day Ethical Protector Course to the rest of the department—25 officers at a time. Quite a commitment! The training included ethics, communication and de-escalation skills (we used the Verbal Defense & Influence (VDI) methodology), and tactical skills. Every training day also consisted of a PT session where the participants—mentors and officers, alike—worked on fitness and shared the adversity together. There we bonded and had some fun. Personality clashes evaporated. We were "one team—one mission" all the way.

3. **Sustainment.** The training was always great for morale, and the officers responded overwhelmingly in a positive way. But we worried about how to sustain the momentum. The mentor program was one way: make sure the mentors followed up with the

officers and informally answered any questions they might have about the tactics or de-escalation techniques. But we realized that we needed a "practice" that could be done, virtually on a daily basis, so that the training wouldn't wear off, and the culture would feed on itself and keep evolving in a positive way. This is not easy. The life of a police officer can be very busy and stressful anywhere, but especially so in a dangerous city like Camden. There are sometimes long hours, and the pay is not always great. It's hard to schedule anything but state-mandated training. Keeping physically fit is also a challenge. But once a culture is established, it can be self-reinforcing.

4. **Our sustainment suggestions: A tool we call "CAP" (Clarify, Activate and Practice).**

   a. *Clarify*. This first step consists of just one thing: re-affirming our self-concept as a protector or guardian of life, no matter what.

b. *Activate.* Moral behavior can be effectively inspired through the emotions. Consistently activate the protector self-concept by sharing stories. And the officers of Camden—perhaps of every city—have stories of heroism and selflessness to spare. Tell them.

c. *Practice* Put everything together with quick reviews of the tactical and verbal skills as a daily practice. This is a commitment but can realistically be done in 5 or 10 minutes at roll call and be led by whichever mentors happen to be on shift. Then call on someone to give their favorite anecdote about a friend or colleague (or even talk about a timely story from the news) that epitomizes the image of an Ethical Protector. Then, do one physical activity. It could be a weapon retention move. Or the unholstering and re-holstering of a weapon 10 times in a row with eyes closed. Or 10 pushups or deep squats. It doesn't have to take long—just a couple of minutes. Get creative! But do it every roll call, and don't leave out the physical part. Don't just talk! To wrap up roll call, instead of saying "be safe," we recommend saying something like, "remember, everyone is safer in your presence." Eventually it all will become part of the culture, and that's when the important changes start.

We could probably write quite a bit more, but we think you have the idea. Certainly, contact us if you have questions. But, in summary, with some motivation, a plan, and a sustainment methodology you can improve the morale and effectiveness of your officers, as well as positively impact your officers' tactical and communication skills. The Ethical Protector philosophy also has a good chance of helping you improve your relationship with the community you are sworn to serve.

Another department we worked with that also bears a quick mention is Toms River, NJ PD. Unlike, the new Camden County Police Department, Toms River was well established. They were struggling with excessive demeanor complaints, as well as some unique cross-cultural challenges. But they couldn't just start from scratch. In order to create an Ethical Protector culture, they would have to "change the tires while the car was moving." We suspect many departments would have similar challenges to culture change. Its very hard.

Yet, Toms River used the methods described herein to enhance their culture in real time. The innovative Chief, Mitch Little, has been successful in creating a wonderful new partnership with the community, and the police and the citizens now have established relationships and processes to help them work through community challenges together. Officer morale is way up, also. We are immensely proud of our association with Toms River, they show us what can be done with a commitment to the Ethical Protector concept and effective leadership (by the way, the hospital where Bruce works is in Toms River).

The bottom line is this: Many departments struggle with complaints, morale problems, and maintaining a close connection with their communities. They may also be under intense scrutiny by the media. Having a department of real Ethical Protectors will keep the community supporting you and the media telling the story you'll want them to tell.

Epilogue

So much has happened since we introduced the Ethical Warrior and Ethical Protector concepts to the law enforcement community. The notion of an Ethical Protector grew out of Jack's work with the Marines and Bruce's idea for adapting it for law enforcement. Subsequently, we have had many friends, students, and colleagues from various backgrounds—from law enforcement and military leaders, to philosophers and scholars—who have convinced us that the values of an Ethical Protector are perfectly appropriate for anyone in the public safety professions.

And so, it began. Articles were written and also Jack's book, *The Ethical Warrior: Values, Morals, and Ethics for Life, Work and Service*.

Ethical Protector training courses were arranged and delivered to military personnel, law enforcement officers, park rangers, educators, businessmen, and even medical professionals, including a physician heading to Haiti after the earthquake. The whole process has been wonderful. Undoubtedly, we have learned as much—or more—about being an Ethical Protector from the people we have had the privilege to train as they have learned from us.

And our mission continues. Bruce retired from the FBI and started a new protector career as a hospital security director. Jack has the honor of addressing various groups who ask Resolution Group International to speak to them about the Ethical Warrior/Protector principles. Those groups include the NYPD, Chicago Police Department, New Jersey State Police, the International Law Enforcement Education Training Association (ILEETA), the US Marines, as well as various corporations and universities. They have all been great, but we wanted to tell you about one particular experience Jack had.

Jack recounts:

I was invited to be a keynote speaker at an Ottawa Police Service Ethics Symposium in Canada. The trip started off a bit strangely when immigration stopped me at the border and gave me a hard time about entering the country without a work visa. I explained that I was in Canada as an invited guest of the Ottawa Police Service (OPS). The border agent was unimpressed, and it took several calls back and forth to a representative of the OPS to get it straightened out so I could finally enter the country. I remember thinking, "Geez, this is as bad as trying to get into the United States. What's that all about?"

But things went perfectly after that rocky start. Everyone was warm and welcoming, the presentation was well-received, and the discussions were lively and respectful. But I was struck by the fact that many statements by Canadian participants were preceded with the phrase, "After 9-11" or "Since 9-11."

I thought, "9-11? Why all the talk about 9-11?" It seemed that everyone I spoke with had rearranged their lives, jobs, and priorities because of what had happened to the United States on that day. Huh? Why? This was Canada!

Finally, it clicked. That was the reason for all the security at the airport. The Canadians are not just our neighbors and we don't just share a border with them. They are our friends and allies. And we are not alone in this battle against terror—and crime, for that matter. We can rely on Canada.

Of course, there are other friends and allies around the world who accept as true that killing innocent men, women, and children over an ideology is immoral and unethical. And, certainly, there are other countries that share the belief that criminal activity must be countered competently and fairly. But it is very comforting to know that we have committed and trained Ethical Warriors and Ethical Protectors right upstairs who are on our side. So, God Bless you Canada, and thank you.

We began this journey with a simple question in mind: Would law enforcement officers who behave as Ethical Protectors be safer, healthier, and more effective? Over the course of writing, we have explored various aspects of Ethical Warriorship. We defined the Ethical Warrior and Protector as: A protector of the life of self and others, all others, if possible, including our adversaries. We discussed the philosophical underpinnings: The Life Value of self and others. We clarified our understanding of the meaning of the words "values," "morals" and "ethics," and explored how the Life Value serves as the "true north," pointing us toward life sustaining moral actions.

Our discussion also included more practical aspects: How could law enforcement training be modified to encourage the development of more Ethical Protectors? We looked at the Marine Corps Martial Arts Program (MCMAP) and its integrated mental, physical, and ethical training approach. Leadership and tactics were also examined from an Ethical Protector perspective. We looked at the critical task of protecting our enemies and how that relates to mitigating Post-Traumatic Stress Disorder (PTSD).

We have been blessed with lots of feedback—most of it positive, some negative, but all of it instructive. Perhaps the most passionate comments came in response to the concept of respecting the Life Value of criminal adversaries. They reflected a point of view that is seemingly very logical: "I'll treat criminal suspects/adversaries fairly. I'll limit my use of force to the letter of the law. I'll even call them 'Sir.' But I don't have to respect them." Another reader said, "I respect victims, not criminals."

Fair enough. And that perspective may be enough in the short run. But we believe over time, disrespecting the Life Value of anyone, even our adversaries, can cause problems for us and others. So, we'd like to expand on the discussion of this mysterious piece of the Ethical Protector puzzle. It is the most counterintuitive, but we would argue, also the most important.

What do we mean by respecting someone's Life Value? We don't mean a person's criminal, anti-social, or violent behavior should be respected. We don't mean that criminal actions should be excused because of socioeconomic or other environmental disadvantages, either. We only mean that it is important to acknowledge the value of every human life and to protect that life, if possible.

Not acknowledging the Life Value can cause problems in several ways. People know it when you respect their life. They can see it in your words and actions—even in your eyes. This goes for criminals too. They know you don't respect their behavior, and most can live with that. But if they think you don't respect their very life, by verbally or physically threatening or harming them unnecessarily, they will be more likely to disrespect you back and do what they can to make your job even harder.

Since repeat offenders are an unfortunate reality, they will also be likely to make the next encounter with the law more difficult. It's easy to see how this can lead to a downward spiral. The criminal might be on a downward spiral anyway, but we do not need to make it worse. To the extent that showing respect for the Life Value of an adversary can make them more cooperative, we've made ourselves and our colleagues a little safer.

The most important piece of the puzzle is that being an Ethical Protector is better for us. Protecting our psychological health is an important part of protecting our own lives. We are all part of one human race. When we make the judgment that certain behaviors can negate the Life Value, we make the value of human life a relative value. Quite unintentionally, we diminish the value of everyone's life including our own. We believe this is profoundly damaging to our own psychological health. It is the seed of apathy and burnout.

For those who might insist on taking any argument to its logical extreme, we offer the following question from a critic: "If the authors propose that all human life should be respected, would they respect the life of people like Adolf Hitler and Charles Manson?"

The answer is yes. We would do whatever possible to bring them to justice, even if it meant lawfully killing them, if necessary. We regret that they wasted their lives causing unimaginable pain to others. But we submit that the unspeakable evil behavior of these people still does not separate them from the human race. And that is as far as respect needs to go.

We must be clear in stating the obvious: There is no need to respect or even remotely condone criminal actions. That perspective smacks of the very kind of moral relativism that we must avoid. What we are recommending, however, is a simple philosophical clarification: Behavioral values are relative and are in a totally different category than the Life Value. We can deal professionally, ethically, and legally with criminals' actions and still respect the intrinsic value of their life.

We do not suggest that we have all the answers, only a framework that has proven to help protectors be more effective and healthier. Most readers understand the context of our contention that Ethical Warriorship is applicable to law enforcement. And like most things worth doing, being an Ethical Warrior or Ethical Protector is not always easy, but it can lead to, "a better life!"

About the authors:

Jack E. Hoban is president of Resolution Group International and a Subject Matter Expert for the U.S. Marine Corps Martial Arts Program.

Bruce J. Gourlie is Director of Security at a large hospital and is a retired FBI Assistant Special Agent in Charge (ASAC) and former U.S. Army infantry officer.

About the Ethical Protector Training:

Resolution Group International (RGI) was formed by experienced military, law enforcement and education professionals to provide a specialized approach to conflict resolution and conflict resolution training. RGI's synergistic formula of ethical, verbal, and physical skills is unique. RGI works with the military, various law enforcement and government agencies and corporate businesses to develop Ethical Warriors and Ethical Protectors. RGI's website is **www.rgi.co.**

Additional Reading

The Ethical Warrior. Jack Hoban was shaped by service in the U.S. Marine Corps, a life-changing epiphany at a Cold War bar, and mentorship under two masters. He now delivers a revolutionary view of moral values for our time epitomized by the Ethical Warrior – protector of self and others as equal human beings.

Tie-Ins For Life. Joe Shusko is a retired U.S. Marine officer who has mentored hundreds of Marines, police officers, and regular folk with great success for over thirty years. His secret? He tells them "tie-ins" – stories that inspire moral behavior and an enthusiastic perspective on life. They do more than make you feel good; they are a call to moral behavior.

Values Fort A New Millennium. Robert L. Humphrey was an Iwo Jima veteran, Harvard graduate, and cross-cultural conflict resolution specialist during the Cold War. He proposed the "Dual Life Value Theory" of Human Nature, which can help us: Reduce Violence, Revitalize Our Schools, and Promote Cross-Cultural Harmony.

Available at: www.rgi.co/ethicalwarriorbook/

Made in the USA
Columbia, SC
17 December 2024

49763249R00111